THE
VIRGIN
BANKER

THE
VIRGIN
BANKER

My Life in Finance

Building a business, breaking
glass ceilings and dealing
with dinosaurs

Jayne-Anne
Gadhia

1 3 5 7 9 10 8 6 4 2

Virgin Books, an imprint of Ebury Publishing,
20 Vauxhall Bridge Road,
London SW1V 2SA

Virgin Books is part of the Penguin Random House group of companies
whose addresses can be found at global.penguinrandomhouse.com

Penguin
Random House
UK

First published by Virgin Books in 2017

www.penguin.co.uk

A CIP catalogue record for this book is available from the British Library

ISBN 9780753548462

Printed and bound in Great Britain by Clays Ltd, St Ives PLC

MIX
Paper from
responsible sources
FSC
www.fsc.org   FSC® C018179

Penguin Random House is committed to a sustainable
future for our business, our readers and our planet.
This book is made from Forest Stewardship Council®
certified paper.

To Mum and Dad, supporters always

CONTENTS

CONTENTS

PREFACE

THE YEAR 2016 was one of change for me – personally, politically and professionally.

Some of my closest friends and colleagues have retired from Virgin Money. Our political world has been turned upside down. And both of my parents died within weeks of each other. I don't mind admitting that I struggled to come to terms with it all and to conceive of a new and positive future.

At the same time I was being invited, more regularly than I deserve, to talk to groups of women in financial services about both the Virgin Money story and my own.

Then, in the summer of 2016, Kevin Revell, a friend and colleague for more than twenty-two years, suggested that he would write the Virgin Money story if I could sketch out the outline while on my summer holiday.

On the plane out to the sunshine I started what I thought would be an hour or two of writing. And then the whole thing just poured out and Kevin didn't get a look in.

In writing down the key episodes of my career over the last twenty-five years, three lessons seem to me to be important.

First and foremost, that it is the tough stuff, the difficult moments and the sporadic crises that drive us forward to achieve our dreams. Never give up.

Next, that we need true supporters to succeed. I have been extremely fortunate to have been blessed with some amazing supporters. Above all, Sir Richard Branson has taught me the power of doing good business, finding good people and of saying, more often than not, the word 'yes'!

And finally, just be yourself. Too often we are expected to conform to established norms. But conformity does not always create innovation and growth. We need diversity in business to mirror our society and to be innovative, creative and relevant. Don't do what is expected. Do what you believe to be right.

So, here, in my own words, is my story of being a woman in business and a Virgin banker.

Jayne-Anne

Edinburgh, January 2017

FOREWORD BY SIR RICHARD BRANSON

MY FIRST experiences with banking were not pretty. Back in the sixties, if you were a young person dressed as a hippie, you weren't exactly made welcome inside banks. If you had bare feet, you'd barely make it through the door. Added to that, I happened to be in the record industry, which the bankers viewed with enormous suspicion. Their disdain for the music business was only matched by their distrust of the airline industry, which is where I started my next business. I was treated as an accident waiting to happen, a risk not worth taking. More than once, I had banks threaten to close our accounts and shut down the Virgin brand for good. On one occasion I can still vividly remember, a bank manager came to my houseboat to tell me he was foreclosing on us. I pushed him out of my home and told him in no uncertain terms that he wasn't welcome back. We managed to scramble every last penny we could beg and borrow and survive to fight another day. But back then, if you had asked me what I thought of the people who run financial institutions, my reply would have been short and to the point: 'They are a bunch of absolute bankers.'

Somehow, in October 1997 I found myself in London, dressed up in a bowler hat and pinstripe suit, cutting a red ribbon. We were introducing the world to the Virgin One account. I was officially a banker. How the hell had that happened? One of the chief reasons was the woman standing beside me, all six feet two of her. If I had to name one person who has changed my mind about what bankers are like, and what banking can positively do, it would be Jayne-Anne Gadhia. As you will learn in this book, Jayne-Anne and I are quite different characters, but we have some things in common – a love of people, a sense of humour, a stubborn streak – that have made Virgin's journey into banking one of the most exciting and enlightening rollercoaster rides of my career. Now, they aren't words that you would usually associate with banking, but Virgin Money isn't a normal bank and this isn't a normal book.

The best ideas come out of frustration. I hated the experience of flying with other airlines, where customer service was non-existent and you were lucky to get a lump of cold chicken chucked on your lap. So we started Virgin Atlantic to create a flying experience people loved. If it could be done on planes, couldn't it be done in banks? I always found it silly that bank staff had to sit behind glass windows, making the interaction with customers really impersonal. We're getting rid of the glass in our stores – so that we can get closer to our customers. There were concerns about security, but we worked to address the risks, as we always do. We wanted Virgin Money to feel as close as possible to Virgin Records and Virgin Megastores – places you were comfortable relaxing and meeting friends. Why should the experience of buying a financial product be worse than buying an album? Jayne-Anne and her team soon proved a really obvious point to me that many people missed: the people who work at a Virgin bank aren't really different from the people who run a Virgin record label. They all have the same values, desire to help and sense of fun (though they may have different haircuts!).

Speaking of which, the day we decided to launch Virgin Direct, which went on to become Virgin Money, something was tickling me. It was the idea that the bloke who brought the public the Sex Pistols and *Never Mind the Bollocks* could be the one to sort out their finances too. As everyone left the meeting in the attic of my house in Holland Park, Jayne-Anne asked what was so funny.

'How life moves. One day we're managing the Sex Pistols, the next day we're dealing with pensions. See that seat? Sid Vicious was sitting there not so long ago.'

'Really?' she asked.

'Yes, and you see that corner over there? That's where he threw up.'

Since then, Jayne-Anne has constantly surprised me. From stealing watches to floating companies, from hunting treasure to running marathons, we have been through a lot. One of my favourite quotes I tell fellow London Marathon runners sums it up nicely: 'Don't worry if you fall flat on your face – at least you're moving forward!'

In the future, I am sure that technology will disrupt banking enormously, as it is already changing so many sectors. I am an interested follower of Bitcoin and investor in Blockchain, and while it may not end up transforming finance itself, it will help pave the way. But what I am convinced will not change, no matter how far technology takes us, is the need for personal touches, human interaction and strong, purposeful leadership from organisations. I have started more than 400 businesses for a single reason: to make a positive difference to people's lives. The purpose of Virgin Money, to make everyone better off, is something that really chimes with me. The creation of Virgin Money Giving, which is not-for-profit and committed to making more money for charity, is a great example. I don't just want a bank that makes profit, I want a bank that creates experiences, builds relationships and enriches people's lives. When

I walk into Virgin Money Lounges, where no actual banking takes place, I see people relaxing and talking to each other. I think it's a little glimpse of the future, where business is increasingly online, but only works if it is enhanced through human conversations.

One major change that has to happen in finance is diversification. I was so proud when Jayne-Anne launched her report into women in finance, calling for fairness, equality and inclusion for men and women. It is long overdue: the situation is outrageous, and it has to change. One way progress can be made is by empowering more entrepreneurial leaders to shake things up and screw business as usual. Jayne-Anne is one good example; her partner for the first years at Virgin Direct, Rowan Gormley, is another. He founded Virgin Direct for us, with Jayne-Anne and then went on to build his own wine business, his real passion. He now runs Majestic on the UK's high streets. It is vital to find brilliant people, and then empower them to grow themselves as well as their businesses. By giving them the space to try things and the freedom to fail, eventually they will succeed. That's definitely been the case at Virgin Money.

This is a story of taking risks, making mistakes, celebrating triumphs and learning from successes as well as failures. It's a unique take on a unique world I never thought I would be a part of. It turns out banking without the bollocks wasn't such a bad idea after all. And, as I often tell Jayne-Anne, I'm more than happy for you to call me an absolute banker.

London, January 2017

PROLOGUE

'It's so odd to have all you bankers here. It wasn't that long ago that the Sex Pistols were in here being sick in the corner.'

I T'S A crisp autumn day in 1994, and I've set off from Norwich train station to London, and to Holland Park, a place I've never been to before.

I come out of the tube station, turn left along Holland Park Avenue, and up a slight hill to a row of expensive London townhouses.

Number 11 is on the left as I walk down the street. It's a huge white, double-fronted mansion with a wrought iron porch. Outside are several black Range Rovers.

I can't actually believe that I am going to Richard Branson's house. He's cool and famous. I'm anything but!

I walk up the little stone path with criss-cross mosaic tiles and press the silver intercom to the right of the door. I can smell the autumn leaves and hear, in the distance, the shrill ring of the door-bell. I'm very, very nervous. I'm on my own and have no idea what will happen next.

But a woman's voice comes over the intercom, and she seems to be expecting me. The door swings open – there's no other security – and in I go. I'm expecting to be met but there's nobody there.

I step tentatively into the huge hallway. On the right is a large wooden sideboard with a big carved mirror above it. And underneath, boxes and boxes of white unbranded cans. I'm soon to discover that this is the day that Richard Branson is launching Virgin Cola.

As I look to see where to go, I turn into the living room on the left. It's huge and runs from the front to the back of the big house. I'm taken aback by how homely it feels – big yellow grand piano at the front, huge squashy sofas in creams and lilacs at the back – with big doors leading out into the garden. Scattered among the family photos – and there are many – are little model aeroplanes, all customer service awards for Virgin Atlantic.

There's still nobody around so I walk back across the hall into the dining room. There's a big oak refectory table in it with benches down both sides. You could have a lot of people for lunch there.

On the floor, propped up against the walls, are framed pictures. I especially notice a framed letter from Princess Diana – and the platinum album of *Tubular Bells*!

I venture upstairs, towards the faint buzz of people talking. By the time I get to the third floor there are photocopiers on the landings, and people – cool, young people – rushing about – there's a general feeling of excitement.

At least three of the bedrooms have been turned into offices. It amuses me that one of those rooms is the headquarters of Virgin Brides.

Finally, a young girl comes to rescue me and points me up to the very top, attic floor, where there is a full-size snooker table as you emerge from the stairs. To the left, and in the eaves looking over the back garden, is a separate table and a flip chart.

And that's where we start to discuss the business that will become Virgin Money.

Chapter 1

EARLY TIMES

'You don't want to know what this lot are saying about you.'
'Grandad seems okay,' I said.
'Grandad's blind. He doesn't know you're white.'

Fighting Back

MY JOURNEY to the attic in Holland Park that autumn day in 1994 had been an accidental one.

I was the only child of a working-class family who were determined to better their lot – my parents sacrificed much to give me a good education and I did well at school, where I was good at the academic stuff, but dreadful at games and singing and drama. I had grown too big from an early age (I was over six foot tall by the time I was fourteen), and felt awkward in almost every situation.

I started out in an all-girls' school in Worcester but, when my father lost his job, we moved to East Anglia and my parents dug deep and enrolled me in Culford School. This had traditionally been an all-boys' school, but I was one of the first seventeen girls who joined as the school went co-ed.

The four years that I spent at the school were a pretty brutal experience. Instead of the organised structure of the girls' school, I remember tables and chairs in heaps in Portakabins, and having to fight for your seat in most classes.

Given my gender, size and awkwardness, I guess it's not surprising that I was the butt of many jokes from the teenage boys, who used to hide around corners and scream in horror when I appeared. Of course, because my parents struggled so much to send me there (and my mother reminded me of that frequently), I couldn't tell them about the bullying. And as an only child there wasn't really anywhere else to turn.

So I just sort of dug in, kept my head down, and fought back when the need arose.

I ended up loving the school (although I got screamed at until the very day I left!) and learning a lot. But probably the best lesson of all was never to give up and never to let the bullies win.

I was young for my year at school, so I finished A-levels in history, English and French when I was seventeen, and took a year off before heading to university in London.

I got a job, on the very day I left school, at the Unemployment Benefit Office (UBO) in Diss, Norfolk. I worked there until the day before I left for university, and worked there during every break – from the day the holiday started until the day we went back.

This was 1979, and the number of people out of work was beginning to increase. Sadly, some of the few areas that were expanding and recruiting were benefit offices. I found myself dealing with claimants from all manner of backgrounds, many of whom had found themselves out of work for the first time in their lives. In many ways, the UBO was a better education than university.

I was on 'fresh claims', which meant taking the details of people who had newly lost their jobs and who were 'signing on' – literally signing a piece of paper to say that they were unemployed. I had to fill in a form called a UB210 for every new claimant, and then fill out another form, a UB40, so they were registered on the system and then received the money they were due.

The actual process was quite satisfying, although as I look back on it now I feel positively ancient. You filled in the form on the left as normal. On the right, you had to translate the form details into computer speak, and then, in my case, pass the form to Yvonne in the machine room, who would enter the computer language into another machine that spat out a long, white, snake-like length of paper, about two inches wide, with punch holes representing the code. Then you would feed the punch tape into another machine to transmit it to a central office somewhere for processing.

I loved it. But what I loved most was meeting the people who came to claim and to be paid.

I especially remember (and don't forget that I was only seventeen) being told never to speak to any of the claimants out of the office – and certainly never to give them money.

But one day I had signed on a young, grubby, cheeky lad with blond hair and freckles. We'd had a laugh together, and he was definitely trouble.

A few days later I bumped into him in town. 'Hello, love,' he said. 'I've run out of money and I just fancy some fish and chips – can you lend us a fiver?'

Of course I shouldn't have done. But of course I did. Even though I would have been sacked if the office found out. And that would have been a problem, as I was giving my mum almost everything I earned as rent. So I worried about it. A lot.

Then, about a month later, in the middle of the afternoon, the lad came into the UBO and asked to see me. Quietly, he gave me my £5 back.

'Bet you thought you'd never see that again!' he said. 'But I really needed it. So this is a thank you for trusting people like me.'

And I have, ever since.

University of Life

I went to Royal Holloway College, University of London, to study history. I've always thought it an underrated subject. In the end, human behaviour seems to be at the centre of everything – and it has never really changed, despite our changing times.

But it wasn't the history lessons that changed me at university. It was the people, the experience and the independence.

I didn't really want to go as I was enjoying work at the UBO. But I knew I had to go, not least to satisfy my parents. Like most freshers, I turned up early for the first term and found myself in halls of residence made of breezeblock, and where the freezing communal bathrooms had that crunchy, greaseproof paper stuff for loo roll. That first night everyone headed for the bar and almost everyone was feeling down.

The surroundings – all being grey blocks – were pretty depressing and everyone was a bit homesick. There was a girl there, Sandie, who was particularly upset, and I was comforting her while some of the more senior students were playing snooker. They were all Indian. And one of them was to become (and still is!) my husband.

A couple of days later, it was the freshers' disco and I was surprised to see one of the Indian snooker players – Ash – on the door as a bouncer. We were chatting when the local skinheads arrived, trying to get into the party. Ash threw them out and I remember being rather impressed!

Not long after, Ash and I were in the Chinese takeaway in Egham. Just as we got to the counter, he said to me: 'Just do what I say – turn round, walk out and then run like hell!'

Charlie, the leader of the local skinheads, had come in looking for trouble. It was the first time that – awkward or not – I ran properly fast!

Colour Blind

After that, I moved in with Ash and was introduced to Indian culture. Don't forget, this was over thirty-five years ago and mixed relationships – let alone mixed marriages – were the exception, not the rule.

There are lots of things that, looking back, are hard to believe. Until I met Ash I had never peeled a clove of garlic or tasted a mango. I had never contemplated a view on life different to my own. And I had certainly never come across the idea of arranged marriages.

Ash would disappear from time to time to see potential wives. But our lives together would carry on as normal.

He was two years ahead of me at university and so, at the end of my first year, he left and needed a job. He was able to get one at the UBO in Norwich – and to live with my parents.

One weekend my dad was working away. He was a refrigeration engineer at the time and was working in Hungary. Ash brought my mum down to college for the weekend. We went out and about in London and had a lovely time.

When Ash and my mum got home, they found that the house had been burgled. And not just burgled, but well and truly burgled.

Everything portable had gone. The house had been trashed. And there was human shit where you'd never hope to see it.

Just as Ash and my mum were trying to deal with that, his mum called and he told her what had happened.

'We're coming up,' she said.

'You can't,' he replied. His family had no idea that he was living with my parents – and an arranged marriage still loomed.

To cut a long story short, Ash told his parents about me. They disowned him for about an hour. Then they rang back and said, 'Bring her here tomorrow.' I have never been more terrified in my life.

So off we went in our bright blue Ford Escort. Brown furry seat covers and dice hanging from the rear-view mirror. I kid you not.

And we arrived in Hounslow to meet the family. The house, I remember as spotlessly clean and very white. There was an enormous number of people there, all talking a language I didn't understand – very loudly!

I sat on a soft chair and two of my husband's young cousins came to sit on my lap. They were about two and five years old. Ash's grandad was there too.

The eldest child said to me: 'You don't want to know what this lot are saying about you.'

'Grandad seems okay,' I said.

'Grandad's blind,' he replied. 'He doesn't know you're white.'

And so started my introduction to the rich and varied Indian culture that I have come to know better and love even more. But it didn't come easy and there have been some embarrassing moments along the way.

In 1987 Ash's brother Hitesh married Anita in a full Hindu wedding ceremony. As soon as we arrived, Ash and I were separated into male and female groups. I was the only English woman there. I didn't understand the Gujarati language and never before had I experienced the customs and costumes of a Hindu wedding. I remember clearly that I was wearing a blue matching top and skirt with white flowers all over them. The outfit was a world away from the colourful wedding saris of the beautiful, petite Indian women who were dancing in a room where Anita, soon to be my sister-in-law, was sat in a lovely chair, on a platform, in her heavy wedding sari, with henna hands and weighed down with gold jewellery.

I was feeling awkward, as usual, standing head and shoulders over the rest and not having a clue what I was doing. Imagine my discomfort, then, as the chant went up: 'Janey, Janey, Janey.' It took me a moment to realise they meant me. I was pushed to the front of the room by the platform where Anita was sitting.

An aunt came forward, bearing a silver tray upon which was a small pot of red paint, some brown nuts and a bowl of granulated sugar.

The chanting got louder and the language got more and more confusing. I had no idea what to do until I realised that the bowl of sugar must surely be some sort of confetti.

I took a handful, and, I'm not joking, I threw it over Anita. It was only when everyone screamed that I realised that I had done something terribly wrong. I should have taken a few grains of sugar between my thumb and forefinger and placed them on Anita's tongue as a sign of sweetness between sisters-in-law. Instead, Anita had to go through her long wedding ceremony sticky and glistening with granulated sugar.

I was furious with Ash. 'Why didn't you tell me what I was supposed to do?' I hissed when we were next together.

'I didn't know,' he said. 'I've only ever seen the men at weddings!'

Thankfully we all laughed it off and Anita and the family forgave me. Which was good since Ash and I had married on 5 May 1984.

We had already bought a two-up, two-down house with an outside toilet in Norwich. An old lady had lived there and the stairs were boarded off. No one had been upstairs for over twenty years.

Dinosaur Park

It was from 133 Bull Close Road, Norwich, that I walked to and from work at Ernst & Whinney – which later merged with Arthur Young to become Ernst & Young, now EY – and where I trained to be a chartered accountant.

I hated it.

I had signed up to Ernst & Whinney to be with Ash. He already had a job in Norwich and I needed a job too.

As a historian, it wasn't immediately obvious what I might do, but accountancy in Norwich offered a way forward – and £4,250 a year – which we needed to pay for the house, which had cost us £13,000.

Accountancy launched me into another unfamiliar world. To start with – the senior people swore a lot.

I remember (because we had literally no money, having bought the house) that we were cooking over a camping stove and I bought a pot from Oxfam that was in three parts. That meant you could cook your meat, vegetables and potatoes on one source of heat. When I brought it back from Oxfam I suffered a loud and lively diatribe from Nigel – one of the senior managers – for bringing Ernst & Whinney into disrepute. Apparently, if you worked there, you did NOT shop at Oxfam!

We couldn't afford a dining-room table either, so we took a door off its hinges (it was bright blue on one side and bright pink the other) and ate on that, even if we had guests.

But the worst part of working at Ernst & Whinney, in those days, was the racism.

One of the senior managers at the firm refused to sign my wedding card 'because you are marrying a Paki'. Talk about the University of Life.

Being bullied at school gave me an understanding of how best to react, and I guess that prepared me for the sort of bullying that I found myself dealing with later in life. If anything, my experiences at school also taught me never to accept the taunts and jibes. Fight back, every time, became my motto.

Chapter 2

PART OF THE UNION

1987–1994

'Our boss is livid.'
'Who's your boss?' I asked.
'The Chancellor of the Exchequer,' she said.

Making a Break

STUDYING FOR accountancy exams was horrible. It was a completely new world to me. I went through the first two years fine but failed the third year first time. It was the first thing I had ever failed in my life.

To my surprise the world didn't turn upside down. My husband still loved me and the sky was still blue. I realised that exams were not the be-all and end-all of a successful life.

During my time at Ernst & Whinney we had been the auditors of Norwich Union (NU) and I had been on the audit team. Every so often we would gather at our Norwich offices and always, absolutely always, criticise the managers at NU for what they were doing and for what they had done.

I remember thinking, at those sessions, that I didn't want to be someone criticising the clients. I wanted to be someone who made the decisions – even if I would be criticised later.

The people at NU seemed to like me, so I decided to try and move from Ernst & Whinney to Norwich Union. No one had ever done that before. But, in 1987, I was allowed to go to NU as the new accountant for their unit trust business. (Unit trusts are investments that allow customers to choose where their money goes in units of stock exchange securities.)

Norwich Union in 1987 was an institution, in more ways than one. It had a fascinating history – it was founded in 1797 by Thomas Bignold as a mutual company, one that would share profits with its customers. Its initial purpose was to protect customers from fire – it had its own fire engines that could only be used by Norwich Union customers, who lived in what was, essentially, a wooden city.

Bignold went on to provide policyholders with robbery protection, primarily for the perilous merchant journey between London and Norwich. Later, in 1808, he formed the Norwich Union Life Society, which became an even bigger business.

From those early entrepreneurial roots, it grew from strength to strength, and by the time I joined it employed 4,500 people in Norwich alone. If you joined NU from school, you were pretty much guaranteed a 'job for life', and I worked with people who were the third generation of their family to work in the business.

Clearly this had an impact on the culture of the organisation, and it was generally seen as a very safe and stable company, rather than one that was going to set the world on fire. It did, however, have some great and creative people, as I was soon to find out.

Initially, working at NU was an odd experience. We had worked very hard, in the early months of 1987, to launch a new range of unit trust funds. But, in October, Black Monday hit, and investing in any new type of security was definitely off everyone's agenda.

At that point, employees were still clocking in and out of NU, contracted to do a 37.5-hour week. With the new business launch delayed, the small accountancy team that I led had finished its work by 11 a.m., and we were bored – big time.

One Christmas I went to see my boss to wish him well, and he said to me: 'You're not coming back here in the New Year.' My immediate thought was that I was being sacked. But he continued, 'You've complained so much about the sales and marketing team and what a bad job they're doing – I'm sending you to sort it out!'

I'm Only an Accountant

I was both terrified and chuffed to bits. The job came with a company car as I had to be on the road a lot. That was definitely going to be an improvement on our tatty Vauxhall Astra estate. But I had no idea about sales or marketing.

So, as soon as I got back to work, in a different building, with different people in Norwich, I went to see the Sales Director – a guy soon due to retire – called David Everitt.

'How on earth do I do a good job in sales and marketing?' I asked. 'I'm only an accountant.'

At that time, Norwich Union sold its business through independent financial advisors – IFAs – and they made the difference between feast and famine for the company.

'It's easy,' said David. 'Get out there and make people want to do it for you. Go and build relationships with these IFAs, so when they have a piece of business to sell that's a unit trust, they'll put it with you.'

So I spent a year 'on the road' in my new company estate car, driving the length and breadth of the British Isles, and meeting IFAs everywhere.

Much to my absolute astonishment, by the end of that year sales in the unit trust business had gone up 800 per cent. That was due to a lot of miles driven, but also because I was exposed to two new ways of thinking.

First, in Investment Marketing, I met a wonderful man, full of wit and energy, called Tony Wood. He was a brilliant communicator and helped me properly to understand the products I was selling. It sounds obvious, but with a really clear level of product understanding, it made my job both easier and safer – not selling the right product will always end in tears.

We spent a lot of time on the road together and had a lot of fun and a lot of meals – one evening, in a hotel in Sheffield, we were offered a brandy, in a beautiful bottle, called Louis XIII. We decided to have a glass each before realising that they cost £60 each. (It's a lot more expensive now.) We put it on our expenses – and have both felt guilty ever since!

At around the same time I was also selected to go on a course, run by the Tom Peters Group, called 'The Leadership Challenge'.

I can't remember now where it was held, but I do remember driving a long way on my own and wondering what I was going to find when I got there.

I found a group of international students of about my own age – all feeling as nervous as me – and three instructors: Richard King, Madeleine McGrath and Mike Peckham.

The point of the course was to demonstrate that everyone has individual strengths and weaknesses but, if you know yourself and model the way, you can lead people to achieve the things that you think should be done. Richard and Madeleine led the classroom activity and Mike managed to coerce us into some outdoor activity that filled me with dread. I had never climbed or abseiled before, and I think if I'd known that was on the cards then I might not have turned up!

There was, however, a clear connection between the mental and physical tests as a 'leadership challenge' – it was a really clever way of getting people to think creatively about how behaviour shapes leadership performance.

At the end of the three days everyone had to give a speech on their vision for the future. It was recorded so that we could listen to it on the way home.

I had learned a lot about myself while I was away but when I played my 'vision speech' in the car on an audio cassette (remember those?!) on the way home, I could hear in myself something I had not realised before – that I genuinely had a passion for changing the world around me, and that I could communicate that surprisingly well.

With all of these new lessons and experiences going on, I was becoming pushier at work. I was good at networking and, if I had a spare half hour, I'd go and talk to people all over Norwich Union – just to find out who they were, what they were doing, and sometimes just to have a good old gossip. It soon meant that I knew lots of people and that I was well known around the place.

That was probably the reason that I was approached for a new job after that first year in Marketing.

NU had been looking for a 'Business and Finance Manager' for their Appointed Representative sales force, which had run into trouble. They needed someone to go and see sales agents who were no longer independent. These were 'tied agents' who could sell only NU products. NU needed to help these agents with their finances and also with compliance, as a new world of regulation was starting to unfold.

The biggest problem was that the agents relied entirely on NU for their cash flow. They had been asked to estimate their future sales so that NU could pay them 'advanced commission'. In hindsight, of course, it's obvious to see what troubles that would create. Almost every agent overestimated their sales and, as a result, almost every single one was in debt to NU.

My job was to work out which agents would deliver against their plans. And for those who wouldn't – to get the money back.

I worked for a wonderful Irish boss – Sean White – who had kissed the Blarney Stone for sure. He worked hard, enjoyed a fine glass of wine, would put a bet on raindrops running down the window – and loved Manchester United with a passion that I caught and which has never left me.

One of my team was an equally wonderful man who was, apparently, the absolute opposite to Sean. On the face of it, he was as miserable as sin, as thin as a rake, a vegetarian – and he supported Manchester City. His name was Geoff Walker, and I was terrified of becoming his boss: he was fifty and I was thirty – and a woman, after all. But when it was announced that I was getting the job he brought me a big green apple – typically kind and ironic all at the same time – and told me that I needn't worry. He had only one ambition at the age of fifty, and that was to see out 120 more pay days.

Life in the Appointed Reps team was beyond crazy – as you might expect when you're the person checking people's business plans and possibly taking 'their' money away from them.

Most agents were fine to deal with and appreciated the help, but the more difficult ones were *very* difficult. So we employed a debt collector to go round to see the most truculent agents with me. His name was Jeff (and he travelled with a minder called George who had a body shaped like a wedge) and he was larger than life in every respect.

I hated going out and about with these two but the very fact they were there behind me – with barely a word spoken – meant that the more challenging agents quickly put in place a repayment schedule, and stuck to it.

In the end, we got the good agents back on their feet and the others sorted out so that they couldn't give poor advice and so that they repaid their debts.

At about the same time, Norwich Union was setting up a Direct Sales Force. Allied Dunbar had been successful with a model that saw salespeople working to sell investment and insurance products and being paid commission to do so. They had no salary and so the view was that they would be hungry to make the sale. So Norwich Union decided to bring in a team from Allied Dunbar to set up their sales force.

The trouble with it, of course, was that Norwich Union's culture, which had struggled even to deal with Appointed Representatives, had no idea how to handle a commission-hungry direct sales force.

At the same time, new regulations, through the Investment Management Regulatory Organisation (IMRO) and Life Assurance and Unit Trust Regulatory Organisation (LAUTRO), had come into force to make sure that such teams were fit and proper to sell financial products to the public. Consequently, there was a requirement for extensive individual vetting of new sales people and also for a training scheme that fully documented the competence of every individual in the team.

At Norwich Union the team had grown to 1,000 people nationwide very quickly, and corners had been cut. Of the team, 800 were agents actively selling, with the remaining staff providing support and oversight. That turned out to be an efficient ratio in terms of sales, but not necessarily for control of the business.

There was a lot of concern that recruitment files and training records were incomplete – and LAUTRO was due in to review them towards the end of 1993.

It was decided to merge the Appointed Reps channel with the Direct Sales Force at about that time, and Geoff and I worried about what on earth could be done to get all of the regulatory requirements on the straight and narrow.

In November 1993 Ash and I had our first-ever long-haul holiday. We went to Jamaica and had a wonderful time.

When I came back I was given a huge room with a big desk and told that I was now Business and Finance Manager of the Direct Sales Channel.

And it was at about that moment that the madness started.

Can You Help Me?

When I came back from that holiday in Jamaica, the business was reeling from a visit from the regulators. Files had been checked. Managers interviewed. Sales people questioned.

NU's Head of Compliance, John McDonnell, was stressed and nervous at what could come out – but we turned our attention to sorting out the issues we were clear on, and at least putting new processes and procedures in place. I had hired a new member of my team, Roland Russell, to help me with management information so I could at least see what 1,000 people were doing with their time.

But then, in March, an eerie gloom descended upon NU and I was called in to see the Chief Executive of the Norwich Union Life Society – Philip Scott.

I had known Philip for some years. He had trained as an actuary, a profession that prides itself on the intelligence and cleverness of its members. Philip was certainly very clever but, due to the untimely death of his father, he had never gone to university. So making CEO was a very big deal.

Philip was a maverick, for sure, and liked people to know that. He had a big house and lots of land in Norfolk and every year he would hold a weekend party, where Ash and I, and countless others, would go and collect apples from his orchard and make gallons of cider in the old-fashioned way. It was back-breaking – but any pain was soon soothed by too many glasses of the previous year's output!

He used to love sailing, too, and always had the ambition to retire at fifty and sail around the world. In reality, Philip left Aviva, as NU had become, when he was fifty-five and sailed across the Atlantic in 2014. I am sure he is planning still more big adventures.

On this particular day, Philip asked me to go and see him in his very posh office in the even posher Marble Hall, which was the NU headquarters at the time. Entering into the Marble Hall is an experience in itself. You walk past enormous statues of the company's founders, up some stone steps and through some dark wooden doors into a huge room, lit from above by an enormous glass dome.

Everything hits your senses at once when you walk in – the alabaster ceilings, the mosaic floor, and the walls and forty pillars all made from fifteen types of marble. This building was definitely built to make a statement. In the 1990s this was very much a male bastion (it didn't even have ladies' toilets!) so I found it pretty intimidating to be summoned there.

When I got to Philip's room he was holding a letter from Kit Jebens – then head of LAUTRO – addressed to Alan Bridgewater, who was Chief Executive of the whole Norwich Union Group.

The letter, personally topped and tailed in black ink (it was signed 'Yours ever, Kit', which I thought rather odd given the maelstrom it unleashed), closed down the Norwich Union Direct Sales force for failing to meet regulatory standards. The fact was that

Norwich Union simply could not demonstrate that its sales force was competent to give regulated financial advice.

And then I found that a very strange thing had happened. Every one of the senior managers responsible for the disaster had vanished. Some had gone off sick. One had gone to Spain. Others just went missing.

So Philip asked me to take control, sort out the problem and get the sales force back on the road. I was thirty-two and had never done anything like it ever before.

'Whatever you need,' he said. 'Just ask. And just get it done.'

So I went back to the huge room with the big desk and brought a few people into my confidence – the problem wasn't yet public knowledge. Of course, I talked to all of the people I had met through the years of networking whom I thought could help. Roland and Geoff were at the heart of it all.

Once we had worked it all out, it turned out that none of the sales force could earn a penny until they had all been retrained and re-tested. And that meant testing them, properly and thoroughly, on industry matters, NU products and sales skills.

All of the tests had to be newly written and independently accredited to be of the right standard. Every test had to be documented (we videoed the sales skills) and every person had to pass every test in no more than three attempts. And everything had to be subject to a new Training and Competency (T&C) scheme, which had to be signed off by the regulators. It was a Herculean task.

To keep control while the problem was announced, we decided to send two people to each Norwich Union Direct Sales branch around the country. There were thirty-six branches.

I sat down that first night with the Head of HR and went through lists of people who might be up to the task – whatever their job, their status or their experience. This was just about people who would do their duty, had the right attitude and would care about their work, and whom I had met along the way.

That afternoon I contacted them all and asked them to come in to Sentinel House, home to the investment arm of Norwich Union, next morning, very early, with packed bags – ready to go wherever they were sent.

To my surprise every single person turned up. Some had packed swimsuits in the vain hope that they had won some sort of surprise holiday! But, as I explained to them, it was going to be a tough gig. Sales people were going to lose their ability to earn overnight – and at the same time going to have to train hard, learn more and prove their competence.

Everyone said they were prepared to go – and they went there and then to their allocated branch.

That day the issue was made public. It was the headline on all of the news channels. And next morning it was discussed in the House of Commons. Big names like Donald Dewar and Peter Lilley weighed into the debate, Dewar describing the 'frightening statistics' of non-compliance across a number of financial companies.

The Norwich Union story was part of a bigger and more painful story than most. As the *Financial Times* (*FT*) put it: 'That a blue-chip company like Norwich Union has been compelled to take such draconian steps hints at the true extent of the problem.'

The news made the front page of the *FT* that day, and only the trials and tribulations of Prime Minister John Major, in one of the most turbulent periods of his time in office, prevented it being on the front page of all the other nationals.

I realised that I was right in the middle of a very big problem indeed.

I had been asked to see the regulators next morning and Philip Scott took me down to London in his chauffeur-driven car. The regulators, LAUTRO, were then based in the Centre Point building, which is situated where Oxford Street meets Tottenham Court Road. Philip dropped me off and I went into that meeting with some trepidation. But the reception I got was even worse than I had expected.

A group of people sat around the table waiting for me. As soon as I walked in, I could feel the really hostile tension in the air. I decided to head off the issue directly, and asked what was wrong.

'*Your* boss,' said their leader, Joy Terentis, 'has done an interview in the *Financial Times* today. He says that the sales force will be back on the road on 24 April. That's only a month away. It's impossible. And he hasn't even discussed it with us. It's that sort of arrogance that got Norwich Union into trouble in the first place. And *our* boss,' she continued, 'is livid about it.'

'Who's your boss?' I asked.

'The Chancellor of the Exchequer,' she said.

With a sinking heart, I just said the first words that came to mind. 'Well, I've been asked to do this. Can you help me?'

The atmosphere changed immediately. 'If you really mean that,' she said, 'we will.'

And they did. And I learned two things that have stayed with me ever since. Firstly, be open with regulators and you will benefit from a positive relationship. And secondly, never be afraid to ask for help.

Philip gave me a lift home. I said that I thought it was asking too much to get everything done in just a month. I expected him to have some sympathy. He had none.

'I expect you to get at least 100 sales people back on the road on 24 April,' he said, 'otherwise you will have failed, and you will have to take the consequences.'

It was unfair – but it did the trick. A month later we had 345 people back on the road. A new scheme written. All documentation in place. All the 'i's dotted and all the 't's crossed.

Record keeping was absolutely key, and we had to store video recordings of each person demonstrating their sales capability, so Roland rented a lock-up garage, installed shelving, and made sure that every recording was accessible.

It was a truly mad time. I slept on the floor under the big desk. We lived on pizza. We worked twenty-two hours a day. But we did it.

After that, I was pretty sure that I would get rewarded with a new, big job. I hoped they would make me Sales Director of the resurrected Sales Force. But Philip took me out for dinner and told me I was not going to get that job because, as he said: 'You lack two of the qualities needed to run a sales force.'

'What are they?' I asked.

'A thick skin and bullshit,' he said.

I can still feel the disappointment today – not because I did not get the job, but because NU still had not learned the lesson that those sorts of behaviours are the last ones you need to run a sales force – or any sort of business for that matter. To make matters worse, one of the senior men who had taken no part in resolving the crisis when it started got the job. And very pleased with himself about it he was, too.

There was also an undercurrent of sexism behind that sort of decision. While Norwich Union was no worse than any other big organisation in financial services, the women holding down senior positions were few and far between. Perhaps, for whatever reasons, we were considered 'higher-risk' appointments.

Philip knew I was disappointed. 'I'm not going to give you just any job,' he said. 'Take your time and work out what you want to do and I'll do my very best to support you.'

And so started a very strange few weeks in my life. I had been in the thick of things and leading a critical project which, if it had gone wrong, would probably have brought NU down. Now I had nothing. No job, no office, no desk, no budget, no credibility. I remember clearly a number of people who had been so friendly while I was seen to be doing well just dropped me like a stone.

So, once I had picked myself up, I set off to work out what to do next – and to hold Philip to his promise.

Hello!

Henry Ford once said: 'When everything seems to be going against you, remember that the airplane takes off against the wind, not with it.'

The wind certainly felt against me as I tried to work out what to do after the retraining programme at Norwich Union.

Looking back, I had defined myself based on what job I did and what status I had at work – rather than who I was. And once the job was unclear and therefore the status had gone, I was definitely flapping about in the wind!

I spent some time on a tedious project making life insurance compliant with new regulatory processes. The job was difficult and dull. But I met a whole new bunch of colourful people. One of them was an eccentric, self-opinionated and ultra-fit runner called Judy Brown.

Philip Scott had brought Judy into Norwich Union to lead this huge, technical piece of work, given her success on other big projects at places such as the Post Office. She was self-employed and did one big project for about six months a year, then trained pretty much full time for marathons for the other half. She started the London Marathon with the elite women for many years.

She brought high emotion and high (and positive) stress to the programme – and a new way of looking at things. She worried a lot about 'the culture' at Norwich Union – a concept I had never really thought about until then. It was clear from working with Judy that her self-definition was very different to mine. And, because of her varied influences, she had a much richer outlook on life than me.

Over the previous couple of years, and given my rather vague career path, Norwich Union had agreed to sponsor me to study for an MBA.

I didn't fancy a traditional textbook MBA and so I plumped for a course based on project work. It was run out of the Barbican in London by a professor whose name escapes me – but who looked like an earlier version of Mervyn King. I remember only one thing about him and that was the importance that he put on business relationships: 'Always write and thank people. Always remind them that you exist. Always learn from them. Always make sure that they know who you are.'

It was good advice, and at the same time he introduced me to my MBA tutor Ronnie Lessem.

Like Judy, Ronnie had a completely different view on life than me. He focused very much not on the job we do between nine and five, but on the huge potential to be unlocked if only we could be ourselves at work. He dismissed the idea that we should have a 'work' persona and a 'home' persona, and provoked all his students to find out who they really were and then to bring their true selves to the workplace.

Ronnie had already published a number of weighty books on management theory and practice, and brought an incredible array of influences to his teaching. His work was full of diversity and development. It was anything but a typical learning process.

He came across as nothing if not extremely direct. If you had a creative idea, he would encourage it. But if he felt that you were not giving enough of yourself to something that was important, he would make sure that you knew about that as well. Loudly and bluntly! I had never met anyone like Ronnie before, and he left me feeling that all of us can change the world through ourselves and our businesses.

It was with these new thoughts of business culture and business revolution that I set off one day in August to see a friend who ran an advertising agency in London.

Alastair Gornall was a creative advisor to Norwich Union's Marketing Department. He was Sandhurst educated, had started his career in New York and then returned to the UK, where he launched two very successful PR companies. So he was properly organised – and clever and creative at getting good business communications out to customers, intermediaries, journalists and the wider world.

He was also great fun and liked a good lunch!

He had invited me to meet him at L'Escargot – a posher place than I had ever been before – on Greek Street in London. I can still feel the thrill of going in there, the buzz of people, the white linen tablecloth, and a bottle of Cloudy Bay between us – which I thought was the best thing I had ever tasted.

On the train down from Norwich to Liverpool Street I had been reading *Hello!* magazine, which featured an article about Richard Branson and his way of doing business. The front cover announced 'Richard Branson – At Home on Breathtaking Necker Island'.

Inside, there was a lengthy interview alongside the otherworldly pictures: Richard talked about family, luck and hard work, the importance of fabulous employees, flexible employment, his hope for his children and much more.

Over lunch at L'Escargot, I told Alastair that I didn't know where my career was going at Norwich Union and that I was almost thinking of writing to Richard Branson to see if there was a job for me at Virgin.

'How funny,' said Alastair. 'My friend has just gone to work at Virgin. I'm godfather to one of his children. I'll introduce you to him.'

A few days later I met Rowan Gormley ... and my life changed forever.

Chapter 3

BECOMING A VIRGIN

1994–2000

'Jayne-Anne has just called a bunch of people – not only have they got jobs to do here, we don't think any of them are the right people to set up this business.'

Project Jam Tart

I HAD NEVER met anyone like Rowan.

A year younger than me, he seemed a thousand times more worldly-wise. Tall, handsome, with a goatee beard and piercing blue eyes, his South African accent made him appear quite exotic, and his physical and intellectual fearlessness made him magnetically attractive to everyone he met.

He had a self-confidence I had never experienced before which teetered on – and sometimes fell over into – arrogance. But that was what made him brilliant.

Like me, Rowan was a chartered accountant (you could probably not have imagined two less likely or less alike). He and his wife, Jenny, had come to the UK from Cape Town, and the history and turmoil of his country was alive to Rowan. He loved his country with a passion.

When he came to the UK, he and Jenny had two small children, and Rowan wanted to sort out his family finances for their new life. He couldn't believe that, as clever as he was, he could not understand the plethora of financial products available to him. All he wanted was to make sure that his family was protected if he died, and that his pension was in place if he didn't.

But he correctly spotted that something so important was made opaque by UK products and by many of the advisors who sold them. Pretty much any investment or savings product was sold through advisors or brokers, and, partly because the products themselves were so complex, they were hard to explain and harder to understand.

There were lots of charges, lots of commission being paid and, typically, the products would be managed by a fund manager who was paid to invest competitively against a range of stocks and shares, and not always in a transparent manner.

In 1994, Richard Branson was starting to think about extending the Virgin brand beyond entertainment and aeroplanes. He had been working on a deal with Electra Capital, which was an investment company, and Rowan was part of the Electra team. The deal fell through, but shortly afterwards Richard called Rowan and offered him a job – there and then – to look at new opportunities.

On Rowan's first day, there was a discussion around where the Virgin Group should go next, and there were lots of suggestions around spaceships and hotels, nightclubs and boutiques. Against the flow of the conversation, Rowan suggested financial services. Richard asked why, and Rowan replied that no one trusted banks, and they would probably trust them even less in the future.

Rowan felt that Virgin would be the right brand to cut through the complex world of financial services and to work as a trusted brand. He started to call a number of companies to see if they would be interested in a partnership with Virgin. And, in a moment of serendipity, one of those companies was Norwich Union.

Philip Scott was already excited about the opportunity to partner with Virgin. He had codenamed the adventure 'Project Jam Tart', which he thought an amusing take on the Virgin brand. So when, having met Rowan, I asked Philip to stick to his earlier promise and support me in a new future, he readily agreed and put me on the team.

As we started out, Rowan told me that it was important that we sorted out personal terms. He knew we had a great opportunity and wanted to make sure we got our fair share of the rewards. Although Rowan offered to negotiate financial terms for us both, in the end we decided that he would agree his position with Richard Branson and I would agree mine with Philip Scott.

I went to see Philip and wrestled out of him a £20k pay rise on my £60k salary. I thought I had won the Lottery.

Rowan went to see Richard. When he arrived, Richard was in the bath. Rowan went into the bathroom for the meeting – not something I would have envisaged doing with Philip. With Richard, I presume, at something of a disadvantage, it was agreed that Rowan would get 2.5 per cent of the company.

And there, in a nutshell, was the difference between us. Talk about a gender pay gap.

After a few months of soul- and job-searching following the Norwich Union retraining exercise, I could not have jumped into a more crazy, full-on, exciting, tough and all-encompassing world if I had tried. And I hadn't tried, as I really hadn't realised that such a world existed.

The first few weeks were all about putting the deal together between Virgin and Norwich Union.

My great friend and expensive drinking partner, Tony Wood, joined the team to handle product design and marketing. Rowan managed all of the external relationships, the deal and the financials, and I took on the business build, the operations and regulatory compliance.

And so it was that I made the regular pilgrimage to Holland Park, through the house and up to the attic, where our little team were putting the plans – and the deal – together.

From time to time Philip Scott would join us to see how things were going, and occasionally he would drive me down from Norwich and back again. He would leave the Marble Hall in his normal, formal business attire and we would stop along the way for him to 'dress down' into a Branson-proof open-neck shirt, chinos and a jumper. It was important that he took off his tie as, at the time, Richard would often carry a pair of scissors around with him and separate tie from owner without warning.

So Philip was not exactly being himself at work and he was not exactly aligned with the NU culture either – but it was a good effort. I have always thought of Philip getting changed in a telephone box, Superman style, and I have thought it so often that I can't remember now if that was true or if I made it up. Either way, the transformation was real.

It was hard work for us all, but there is no doubt that Rowan worked the hardest in putting together the deal. It was my first experience of the long, tortuous days and nights of deal making and corporate lawyers – and I didn't realise then that I would have many more of those ahead.

We started to build the plans in mid-October 1994 – just six months after the Norwich Union sales force had got back 'on the road'.

It is hard to imagine now that, back then, the internet didn't even exist, but, given his own experiences, Rowan was very focused on making our products both simple and accessible directly by customers over the telephone, and emulating the low-cost efficiency so recently achieved by Direct Line and First Direct. As a result, we called ourselves Virgin Direct.

As Tony and I had been working for years as part of Norwich Union's asset management business, we were pretty expert on the products and especially the new 'Personal Equity Plans', or PEPs, that the government had recently introduced to encourage tax-efficient saving. A PEP was often described as a 'wrapper' to allow a customer to invest tax free, and take advantage of investment opportunities only previously available to very wealthy clients. But they were quite complex and only available through intermediaries, and therefore many people were just not taking the opportunity to buy them.

So we decided that offering these PEPs widely, over the phone, to the great British public would be the right thing to do for us, and for our customers.

But investing in the stock market can be risky. And there was no guarantee that investment fund managers would deliver a decent return, even before charges had been applied. So we decided that we would launch a 'tracker' – that is an investment product that fully tracks a particular stock or share index and where no active investment managers are involved.

We proved conclusively that, over time, the FTSE All Share Index beat almost every active fund manager, and so we set up our first-ever product – the Virgin FTSE All Share Tracker – to make stock-market investment available to everyone with as little risk as possible. We took out all the hidden charges, and designed a product that was really simple to understand.

As Richard put it: 'My impression of the market was that it was packed with hidden charges, pushy salesman and meaningless jargon. So I put a team together to do it better.'

In other words, our task was to take out all of the things that customers hated about investing. In the end, that made the business design clear, simple and straightforward.

The next big decision was where we should set up our operations. Rowan lived near Crawley, which is where Virgin Atlantic is based, and he had assumed that we would set up our business from there. But I knew that I needed my friends, colleagues and contacts from Norwich Union if I was to make anything happen at all.

So one day I rang him and said so. 'If you want me to do this, it will have to be in Norwich.'

It was a big call for Rowan. He would have to move himself and his family from London to Norfolk. I heard a momentary hesitation in his voice before he said: 'Okay, I'll move to Norwich.'

I don't know how or when he told Jenny about his decision, but we were off. We could start to build our business.

Dinner Time

By 19 December 1994 we had a plan and a legal agreement, and that night our very small team had a dinner together with Richard Branson to celebrate the imminent launch of Virgin into financial services.

We had a private room in a London restaurant. Richard sat in the middle with his back to the door and I sat to his left.

I was thrilled to have the opportunity to talk with him about more than just the deal. Ever since I had been aware of pop culture, Richard Branson had enjoyed rock-star status. The Sex Pistols had shocked a family like mine. Boy George caught our imagination – but the drugs shocked us too. And then there was Mike Oldfield, and Peter Gabriel, and Simple Minds, and the Rolling Stones ... all the big names that I had listened to so intently when I was growing up.

I was sitting on the grass at home in Norfolk in the 1970s listening to Radio 1 on my little caramel-coloured plastic radio when the news came on that Richard Branson had bought an island in the Caribbean. Oddly, I can remember that I was wearing suede multi-coloured shoes and purple cords at the time – about as uncool as you could get. And this rock-star buying an island? Well, that was about as cool as you could get.

So, roughly twenty years later I had to pinch myself as I sat down for dinner next to the man himself and I asked him about buying Necker Island.

I think the story is now well known – but at that point I didn't know that Richard had been trying to impress his then girlfriend by taking her to New York and pretending that he could afford to buy a Caribbean island.

Richard had convinced an estate agent that he was interested in the island, and negotiated an all-expenses paid visit. When they arrived by helicopter, Joan and Richard fell in love with the place, but as soon as the agent heard Richard's offer, which was much lower than the 'discounted' asking price, Richard and his wife-to-be were left to make their own way home.

Richard had put in a very low bid – and some months later, when the island had still not sold, that bid was accepted.

'How did you know you could afford it, get water on it, live on it, get to it?' I asked.

'I didn't,' said Richard, 'but I knew if I worked hard enough then I'd find a way.'

'By the way,' he said, 'what's the time?'

I looked at my wrist to find that my watch was missing.

'Oh – I've lost my watch,' I said.

And we, and others at the table, looked everywhere for it.

After a while, Richard put his hand in his breast pocket and brought out ... my watch.

'Do you mean this watch?' he asked.

I was astounded. My watch is a bracelet – you have to undo a tight clip and slide it over your hand to take it off.

'How did you do that?' I asked.

'I hypnotised you,' he said.

'You can't have done,' I replied. 'I don't believe in that.'

'Nor do a lot of people,' said Richard, 'but I have proof. A while back, we needed to lease some new planes from Airbus but we couldn't afford the asking price and I couldn't negotiate them down. So I asked the CEO of Airbus to dinner to see if we could do a deal.

'The CEO of Airbus was adamant that he would not go lower. So I said, "If I hypnotise you, will you let me have the planes for the price I can afford?"

'"You won't hypnotise me," said the CEO, "so yes, okay."

'We carried on chatting over dinner. And at the end of dinner I asked him the time. He was surprised to have lost his watch. We looked everywhere for it before I produced it out of my pocket.

'"How on earth did you do that?" he said.

'"I hypnotised you," I said. And I got the planes at the price I could afford.'

I knew then that I had entered a new and exciting world where, if you never take no for an answer and have fun along the way, you can achieve amazing things.

When, after dinner, the contract was signed and Norwich Union and Richard Branson each invested £2 million into the newly created Virgin Direct, I was sure that there would be plenty of adventures ahead.

Uncommon People

The first of those adventures was getting the business off the ground. Not long before we signed the deal between Norwich Union and Richard Branson, Rowan, Tony and I were pretty much alone in putting in the long, hard hours needed to get the business up and running, despite the inevitable myriad of advisors that, I now realise, are a feature of any business deal.

Things got better when we signed the deal because we had £4 million with which to work. But that is not much to set up a business – let alone a regulated financial services business.

We needed premises, people, systems, marketing literature, advertising. The list went on and on. Having been the one who insisted on locating the business in Norwich, it fell to me to find the premises.

Around the time of the deal there was some sort of Norwich Union Christmas party where I found myself dancing with Philip Scott.

'Is there a building we can have?' I asked. 'What about the Training School down at Whiting Road? The ground floor would be great.'

And so Discovery House became our home – as it still is today. We were given a quarter of the building and shared it with teams from Norwich Union. Discovery House is a somewhat anonymous office building on a business park, just outside the centre of the city. It is about as far away from the opulence of the Marble Hall as you can imagine.

It didn't have much in the way of perks, although it did have a big basement with a canteen, which was occupied soon after by my great friend Marguerite Akister and her catering team. We didn't know at the time, but keeping people fed and watered, and giving them a place to chat as a break from some of the hours we had to work, would end up as an important part of our culture.

Next came the people. I wanted us to employ those I had worked with and trusted in the previous months through NU retraining and beyond.

I phoned about a dozen people and, sworn to secrecy, asked them not to go to work at their normal jobs at Norwich Union next morning but to come to Discovery House and be part of starting up Virgin Direct. Despite the huge personal risk – there was no job offer, no contract, no business – everyone did just that.

That day, the HR Director from Norwich Union called Rowan. I happened to be in his room at the time and he answered on loud-speaker.

'We're really pissed off here, Rowan,' he fumed. 'Jayne-Anne has just called a bunch of people down to Discovery House with-out any discussion with us. And not only have they got jobs to do here, we don't think any of them are the right people to set up this business.'

To his eternal credit, Rowan said, 'I don't really see what the problem is. If you don't think they're any good and Jayne-Anne wants them, we'll have them – thanks very much.'

And so that first team was built – and importantly, given the attitude of NU's HR department, we now had something more to prove than just setting up a new business.

Geoff – now with less than 120 pay days to go to retirement and constantly surprised to be part of a much younger team – was the grumpy, crotchety and practical Head of Compliance.

Roland – who had joined to help with management information and never, ever ended up in that job even twenty years later – was the dark, brooding presence who built operations – and someone with whom you just did not argue.

Ant Mullan – a former BP oil man who always wanted to change the world and thought first, foremost and from front to back about the customer – designed the business processes.

Kevin Revell – blues singer, songwriter, runner, father, and an intense spirit who could affect a room with a frown – took on IT.

Pete Ballard – handsome, clever, everyone's friend and soon to set up his own successful business – handled project management.

Karen Thornber – who knew everyone, talked nineteen to the dozen and could spot a good hire a mile off – set up our own version of HR.

Helen McAllister – worldly-wise, glamorous, loud, opinionated, driven, determined, ferocious and caring – set up the call centre.

Simon Leeming – a key member of the earlier NU retraining project – had a special mission to build our Virgin training programmes and to execute them well.

Richard Levell – a quiet man with an absurd sense of humour and the ability to get on with everyone – looked after the project finances and compliance operation.

Martin Campbell – quiet, articulate, modest, and very aware of the world around him – took on the task of communications and PR.

Dave Greenwood – a kind and intense project manager – was tasked with looking after the readiness of the business; he would always have 'three things' to raise at the end of any meeting, no matter how long we had been running.

Every day, we got together first thing in the morning and last thing at night as a team to make sure that we were all headed in the right direction to deliver the business we wanted on time and on budget.

And that was no small challenge.

The PEP product we were planning to sell had tax advantages and so customers would usually buy it during March – in the run up to the 5 April tax year end. Inevitably, Rowan and Richard both wanted the business launched by 28 February.

Having signed the deal only on 19 December with no business infrastructure at all and with no regulatory approvals, it was a tall order indeed.

But Richard couldn't understand why. 'We launched an airline in ninety days,' he said. 'How can this be more complicated than that?'

So, off we went to see the regulators. We needed approval from both LAUTRO and IMRO. Both were dubious about Virgin in financial services. 'Virgin is about airlines and entertainment,' they said. 'How can you be ready to enter the regulated world of financial services?'

I remember Richard's answer well.

'There is no more regulated industry than airlines,' he said. 'People wouldn't get on my planes if they didn't think they would get off the other end.'

And with that, and the regulatory relationships I had built through the retraining programme, we were off.

But we still had systems to build – both to process initial applications and to answer calls. It was a complicated build.

Rowan was keen to have a reputable, heavyweight systems provider who could get us an off-the-shelf solution in our timescale. But it soon became clear that such a solution simply did not exist. We went to IBM, Logica, Genesys, Syntegra – they all said it would take many months to build, and at a cost of many millions of pounds, which we simply did not have.

So, Kevin and a new member of the team, Mark Crack, set to work to build our own. It matched our processes and the way we wanted to deal with our customers, and it functioned in a way that our telephone operators (teleops) wanted. So process and system were as one. We could never have achieved that with a ready-made system.

We built it in Lotus Notes. And it cost £17,000.

Meanwhile, we set to work recruiting and training that first team of teleops. We thought we needed forty people for our 24/7 service. All came from agencies as temporary staff – we just did not know if this would work or not – and if it failed we certainly did not have enough money to pay forty people, let alone ourselves, for long.

We recruited for attitude, personality, aptitude and empathy. Resilience also proved to be important to get through Helen's demanding telephone training programmes. Hard work and long hours to get ready for launch were essential. The Virgin name was a great advantage to us in recruiting bright and sparky people who wanted to be part of something exciting. Once we had made it clear that Virgin is not the constant series of parties and free-bies that some had expected, we had a great group of people who were prepared to work hard and have fun at the same time. And that was a combination of skills that was not common in financial service businesses at the time.

Meanwhile, Tony was setting up the new investment funds and writing the marketing literature. 'No hidden charges, no small print, no salesmen' were our key competitive advantages. By proving that '75 per cent of fund managers under-perform the market' we were able to get a strong and clear message across to customers, although it did not make us any friends in the traditional financial services companies.

My L'Escargot friend Alastair was working on the communications plan and we had advertising booked in all the papers.

Rowan had a natural feel for what would work when, and he decided that we should launch to the public on a Sunday. There was a BBC programme in those days called *The Money Programme* and it was very influential. Rowan had managed to get the main slot. All was arranged for us to open our telephone lines and to start business the morning after that programme had aired.

The question was: what date would we make it? By the time people were trained, systems built and regulatory approvals achieved, we launched on 5 March 1995 – less than twelve weeks after signing the deal, but with only three weeks to go until the end of the tax year. Would that be enough to prove ourselves and to prove to the world that the Virgin brand worked in financial services?

We threw everything at it.

On the Sunday night of *The Money Programme*, Richard Branson came to Norwich, while Rowan went to London to appear on TV. The whole team had gathered in our offices to watch the programme together. Rowan's vision of the future came across strongly – positive, inclusive and innovative. He was followed by a downbeat representative from Allied Dunbar, whose view was that sales of investment products over the telephone would never work. Come to think of it, Allied Dunbar haven't been around for years.

Meanwhile, back at Discovery House, there were a couple of speeches and a few bottles of champagne. Richard, ebullient as ever, jumped on a desk and shook and popped a bottle of bubbly to anoint the new business.

Fizz went everywhere – and two of our treasured PCs went up in smoke.

Business Unusual

Richard left at just about the time the PCs stopped fizzing and smoking, and the party wound down. We sent the teleops home but the rest of us stayed to make sure that everything was ready for the next morning.

In what was to become a bit of a tradition in our future releases, we hit some last-minute hitches, and worked through the night to make sure that all the systems and telephony were ready. Just as we thought we were in a good place, an electrician turned up to test the circuits in the computer room. And he pulled out the mains cable and disconnected everything.

Everything we had built went black with only hours to go till launch. None of us had managed any sleep, and tempers were raised. I'm pretty sure the electrician understood that he'd slipped up!

Meanwhile, outside, it had started to snow. Hard. And Norwich does not do snow well. Transport shuts and if anyone wants an excuse not to go to work then there is one right outside their bedroom window.

At 3 a.m. in the morning we still had no working systems and snow was falling at an alarming rate. But we kept our nerve. There were still a couple of PCs out but the system rebooted with minutes to go.

And then we looked out of the windows and down the road from Discovery House. In the dark, with snow falling, at 6 a.m. in the morning, we saw people trudging up the drive and into work. Every one of the team had walked in early. They were there and ready for the start of our big adventure.

They left their footsteps in the snow, stamped their boots as they came into the building, and the first shift sat expectantly at their desks until 8 a.m., when the lines opened.

Nathan Howes took our very first call, the first of an astonishing 40,000 calls on that day, and the phone lines have not been out since.

With only three weeks to go before the tax year end customers flocked to put their money into a Virgin Direct PEP and it was all hands to the pumps. At very busy times everyone got on the phones to take calls and to issue marketing packs out to new customers. I clearly remember one Londoner saying to me, 'Morning, love, can I put a monkey into your PEP?' and realising that I still had much to learn.

We advertised heavily in the Sunday papers, especially those with Money sections. Our ads were straightforward and stood out clearly against our competitors. Although we were open seven days a week, when our phone lines opened at 8 a.m. each Monday morning we would be flooded with calls. Don't forget, this was all new to us and to our customers at the time. We were breaking new ground as a telephone-based financial services company. Among many lessons we learned, one was that customers preferred always to call us from work rather than from home.

And we all got in very early to help in the post room where cheques flooded in every day. An excited shout went up if a cheque came in for £24,000 – the highest amount a married couple could invest for this tax year and the next. Everyone in the management meeting knew how much business had come in each day as they had been opening the envelopes personally.

We put in place a rota for the management team to come in every night, when the telephone lines shut down at 10 p.m. They would make sure the lines were closed, that the voicemail was working and the tapes to record our calls were changed over. Then they would tour the building, closing windows and blinds, and making sure that all the teleops were safe to get home. It never entered our heads to get a security guard to do all of this – it was our business, after all.

By 5 April 1995 we were exhausted, but the new business had exceeded our expectations and we had proven beyond all doubt that the Virgin brand extended successfully into financial services and that it was here to stay.

We had a big celebration, which made me realise what a sheltered life I had lived until then. It was the first of many such parties, and it was about then that we started referring to our building as Disco House! Given that we had recruited so hard on strength of personality, it should not have been a surprise that things got a little lively when we booked out a nightclub and had an unlimited free bar, but we seemed to keep the casualties down to a minimum. In any case, it was these sorts of celebrations that helped to make the

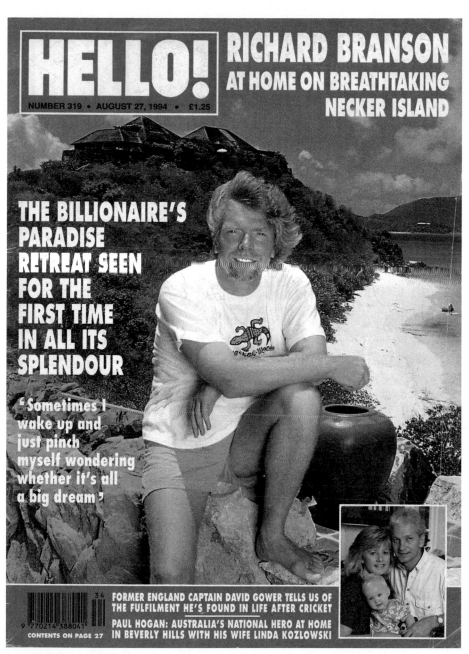

The magazine that changed my life!

Early days at Virgin Direct – Rowan, Tony, Richard and me, 1995.

With Richard at the Stock Exchange, during our first attempt to buy Northern Rock, 2010.

A fun ride for Amy, 2012.

Wilbur Ross, Richard Branson and Jim Lockhart, who later joined our board, celebrating the acquisition of Northern Rock, 2012.

With Dave Bedford and Richard.
Sponsoring the London Marathon in 2008
was really exciting, although the white
tracksuit tops weren't quite my style!

Dave Dyer showing his support, 2011.

Richard Branson, me and Amy at the 2011 London Marathon.

Jumping for joy with Amy, 2012.
My chairman at the time thought this
photo most unbecoming of a banker!

Off to launch the Women in Finance report, 2015.

First Christmas with our new Chairman, Glen Moreno, 2015.

business a really great place to work. Without the free food and the parties, it just would not have been Virgin.

Later on, we were able to reward people with 100,000 Virgin Atlantic air miles for putting in so many extra hours, and, at the end of 1997, we held a raffle for eighteen of our staff to spend a week at Necker Island.

For the people in the business who had previous experience in financial services, the most they might have received as thanks for working hard would have been a free lunch – and while the Virgin rewards were never expected, they made up an unwritten part of the deal. We wanted to be clear that the business realised that people who had been working so hard had been the reason for its success.

The thrill of experiencing a working business that you have built yourself is pretty much unrivalled. And none of us had ever been part of anything like this – pretty much everything had been built from scratch. There was no rulebook that we could follow. The only guidance we allowed ourselves was to copy the good things that our competitors were doing, to ignore the bad bits and to put ourselves in the position of the customer wherever possible.

In some ways, our naivety and challenging approach were the key to success. The reason Richard named his company Virgin in the first place was because of everyone's lack of experience. For us, that meant that we could question everything, and that we had a vested interest in working hard to make the business successful.

Late one evening some time after the launch, I sat with my team upstairs in Discovery House, discussing how on earth we had pulled off such a successful launch in such a short period of time. The business had been so successful that by now we had taken over the whole building.

Everyone took a turn at sharing how they felt now that we had a real business, and two answers stood out for us then and now.

Geoff was quite emotional – which was, in itself, quite unusual for someone who was usually so dry at work: 'The only way I can describe it,' he said, 'is to say that I now realise that all my working life to this point has been in black and white. What you've done is to make me see it in colour.'

Wow! We were all taken aback by his thoughts – and all understood what he meant. But it wasn't what we had done for Geoff – this was something we had all done together.

'No – I feel the same,' said Pete. 'I know that I'm not that great, but what's kept me going is knowing that you all are – and I haven't wanted to let you down.'

Yet again, we realised that we all felt the same – not quite good enough in our own minds to be given the responsibility we had, but pushing on, in colour, supported by people we cared for and respected, never letting one another down.

It was a powerful moment and one that has resonated with me time and again.

Around the same time, Philip Scott took me out to dinner in Norwich to say well done. At the end of the meal he said, 'There's just one thing I meant to ask you. We didn't think the people you took to build the business were up to it. But clearly they were. What did you see in them that we didn't?'

And, although I hadn't realised it consciously at the time, I knew the answer at that moment. We were all the troublemakers. People who were uncomfortable with the bureaucracy and politics of a big business and who wanted to change it. Virgin Direct gave us our chance. And we took it with both hands.

As a result, we built a business that was not just different, it was very different. We had built our own systems and processes, based entirely on what we thought a great customer experience ought to feel like.

We tested the business with many and various possible customer conditions, but we did get caught out when one of our older customers applied for an account. We had not catered for applications from people born in the 1890s!

We had spent hours and hours poring over every piece of customer literature to make sure that it was not just compliant with the rules, but it was easy to understand. We had knowledgeable, articulate and friendly people answering the phone in a way that explained our product consistently and fairly.

And the culture of the business, thanks partly to the lack of hierarchy and of silos, was coherent, engaged and creative. The teleops cared about more than just getting their pay – this felt like everybody's business.

Over the years, there has been a lot of talk about call centres being the new 'dark satanic mills', where workers are repressed in draconian conditions, but this felt anything but that – there was such a positive vibe about the place because people genuinely loved being part of something that was challenging the status quo and succeeding.

Meanwhile, Rowan could see that his vision had created something with great potential and he wanted to extend it far and wide. But Norwich Union wanted more evidence of success before they put more money into growing Virgin Direct further. So, always the deal-maker, Rowan looked for new partners who would invest in Virgin Direct and support our future plans.

As a result, we met with the Australian Mutual Provident Society (AMP). They were looking to expand and had already acquired the Pearl Life Assurance Company in the UK. Virgin Direct could extend that investment direct to consumers through an innovative brand.

As a result, we started a new project – building life and critical illness insurances – and at the same time looked to buy out Norwich Union and introduce AMP as a new partner.

Rowan and I flew off to Sydney to meet the Australians on more than one occasion – sometimes there for no more than a day or two as they grilled us on our plans, the brand, the market and our capability.

And all the time, back home, we had to keep that confidential as we still wanted to see if Norwich Union would put in the money we wanted, and match any deal we could get from AMP.

In the end, AMP won. Philip could not get the support of his Board to go further without more proof that Virgin could really work as a financial services organisation without cannibalising Norwich Union's own customer base. But AMP put the necessary money on the table.

I felt temporarily sad – and scared – at breaking with Norwich Union and letting down Philip – but they could not compete and others could. I wasn't the only one feeling scared. My team, all of whom had come across from NU, were concerned about cutting ties with the company that had provided support, processing and administration to the business.

So we ran a side project to make sure we could survive as a business on our own, without Norwich Union. We had a contingency plan for absolutely everything that we could think of, from infrastructure support to administrative processes and all the way through to food deliveries. Quietly, we went about sourcing alternative suppliers where necessary. It didn't mean that the challenge was any less, but at least we knew where we were exposed. And when the partnership ended, we found that we didn't need a lifeline. We were growing up as a business.

By the time we launched our life insurance products, Virgin had a new Australian partner in Virgin Direct and the demands on the team grew even more challenging as a result.

The next two years were a whirl of new products, and new ways into markets. In addition to life insurance products, we had enhanced the PEP product using a completely new system, launched unit trust investments, and were on track to launch a pensions product by the end of 1996. On top of that, we were keeping the business running smoothly and dealing with the demands of a big Australian shareholder.

There was still much to do but the strain was showing in a number of ways. Rowan and I argued on many occasions about the direction of the business and the speed with which we could build it.

The atmosphere was like a pressure cooker as we all worked together in a small building under intense scrutiny from shareholders, press, customers, regulators and staff at all times. We needed to do more with less. Build new systems. Answer more calls. Hire more people.

Many of the original teleops had shone through those early days and were now on full-time contracts and with bigger, broader roles in the business.

Most notable was Mark Barnes, who had a special gift of understanding people, resolving tensions and creating a positive culture in the business and beyond.

Along the way, Mark sorted out relationships, one-night stands, unwanted pregnancies and abusive marriages, as well as doing his day job. As the business grew, it was as if the family was growing too. And we aimed to build the team as if it was a family – where shared experience bound us tightly together.

Three more members of the team joined us, to lead work on systems, processes and infrastructure:

Richard, a lovely Liverpool funny-man, who lightened the mood and tested the people, systems and processes.

Vince, an intense technical expert, proud of his Spanish heritage, and a great foil for Richard as his team came in to build more sustainable systems on a new platform.

And Malcolm, a larger-than-life character in every respect, whose religious beliefs contrasted with a wicked sense of humour, worked on the strategic direction for our infrastructure.

We continued to have our management meetings at the start of each day and at five o'clock in the afternoon. The five o'clock meeting became something of a ritual. There was no set agenda, other than what had gone into my notebook for the day. Everyone was given *carte blanche* to say their piece not just on their own subject but on others as well, and after that discussion we went around the table to cover any other issues of the day.

As a result, the meetings might go on for three or four hours, and we ended up putting ourselves, and our families, under quite a bit of stress. But it was the only way that we could unify as a team without splitting into functional silos – and losing track of the business direction.

We all went on the Leadership Challenge course that personally I had found so helpful a few years earlier – and learned so much about each other. I renewed my acquaintance with Richard and Madeleine from the Tom Peters Group and with Mike Peckham, who was again tasked with teaching people to challenge themselves both mentally and physically. Abseiling was one of the challenges that we had to conquer. I decided to go down second – after Roland, who was so tough that I assumed he was not afraid of anything. However, as I watched him go over the top, he was ashen. 'Terrified of heights,' he said.

On another occasion, we went on a weekend with the Territorial Army and learned how to camp out together in the woods. One of the team had brought a duvet cover and pillow case so she didn't have to sleep directly in an Army sleeping bag. She refused to go to the loo in the woods until one of the soldiers told her that she was close to the 'ladies' loo'. 'Thank goodness,' she said, 'where is it?' She paled as the soldier gave her a spade.

After that, Mark would put on team-building events with Richard and Madeleine in a Norfolk barn not far from the office, and we would all end up line-dancing together at the end of each day of the event.

The work was harder than anything we had known before; but the satisfaction of what we were able to achieve made it worth it.

I realised that it is impossible to build a financial services product if you don't write the literature in parallel. If you can't explain it simply – it just does not work. And, for sure, you can't have marketing documents that do not line up with operational promises. So we would spend days working out how to explain the product – and what that meant to our processes, our systems and our terms and conditions.

All the time, for some reason, I would eat oranges – and that wonderful smell of fresh oranges to this day reminds me of those long days of product building down at Disco House.

I also realised that the products we were building felt different to me at home than at work. So if, on a Saturday morning, I opened my post and there was a product from a financial services company in there, I realised that I read it differently from the way in which I designed products at work. It was a big revelation and we decided to implement 'the kitchen-table test' for everything we did – a way of building products that customers need and understand, not the ones we want to sell.

That concept has stayed with us through the years and we even have a kitchen table in the Research and Development Lab in our Gosforth offices today.

Making One Day Today

The kitchen-table test worked well for investment, pension and insurance products and it became clear that the Virgin brand could go much further in financial services, without extending products into the realms of complexity. By August 1997 we had £1 billion of funds under management and 200,000 customers. In just over two years we had gone from nothing to being a notable player in financial services.

Rowan was keen to extend our capabilities so that we could give financial advice over the telephone and soon a whole new team arrived to build Virgin Direct Money Managers. It was another ground-breaking moment as those 'experts' who had said that financial products could not be sold over the telephone made it clear that they thought that giving advice was a step too far. And don't forget, the internet still hadn't really arrived yet!

At the end of 1996 we took all the key people in the business off to an anonymous meeting room near Norwich airport to discuss where we should take the business next. We concluded that we should be looking at banking because it was so obvious that the service that most people were getting from their banks could be much better. There wasn't much traditional banking experience in the room, but that had never stopped us before. In fact, it had become very clear that building a financial services business from the viewpoint of the customer made much more sense than repro-ducing what had been done previously.

At the same time, it turned out that a number of the big banks were approaching Richard Branson to suggest joint ventures across a range of banking products.

Lloyds were keen to partner with us in a credit-card venture and we all went down to Southend to see their card operations in action.

There was also interest from Capital One – then quite a new but very successful US credit-card company.

Ant, Vince, Richard and I headed off on a Virgin Atlantic flight to Washington, DC to see the Capital One team. It was our first flight in Upper Class. I slept, but the others enjoyed the bar and the massage. At dinner in Washington that night, I was less than impressed that I was the only one of our team properly awake – we weren't really that used to high-end business travel!

There were a few awkward moments on that trip, where I managed to feel a little out of my depth. One night, I was taken to a posh restaurant with very well-heeled diners. I had my first ever lobster but didn't know how to handle the tools. As I cracked a claw a large portion of lobster shot across the tables and landed on the fur stole of a very posh lady indeed. She was far less amused than were my dinner companions.

Capital One were enormous but had a culture very like our own. Entrepreneurial, data-based, full-on, customer-focused. Although we did not end up in partnership with them, we kept their achievements in mind as we grew.

In the end, it was the Royal Bank of Scotland that came up with a uniquely innovative idea that we thought we could, in partnership with them, make our own.

Dave Dyer and his boss, Frank Kirwan, both working at RBS at the time, turned up in Norwich and presented Rowan and me with an idea for a new type of banking product. Dave later named it 'the Virgin One account'. It was based on an Australian product – the current account mortgage – where a customer would take out a line of credit secured against their home, but reduce the outstanding loan by paying in their savings and their monthly salary and using it for all their current account transactions. Customers could still access their savings and, if they needed to, borrow more money or spend using a linked charge card up to their secured credit limit. It really would be the most flexible account on the market.

RBS were very excited about the product and what it could do for customers. The then CEO, George Mathewson, came to Norwich to discuss the partnership.

Rowan and I met George in Rowan's office in Discovery House for a sandwich lunch. As George got passionately into the negotiation, he bit his tongue – and blood poured everywhere. But he carried on regardless, with blood and words spraying around the room. I knew then that he was one tough cookie!

I asked him why RBS needed us to launch this product and why they couldn't do it themselves.

'We don't have the culture to do it,' he said, 'but you've proved that you can be innovative and successful. And,' he continued, 'if you get it right then I get half the profits. But if you get it wrong – no one need ever know that I had anything to do with it.'

So, a new deal was done.

We found we could work with RBS – they were a relatively small bank then with a good number of hard-working, innovative people who were keen to support the Virgin One account team.

Soon, a new company, 'Virgin One Ltd', was set up as a joint venture between Virgin Direct, which owned 49 per cent of the business, and RBS, which owned 51 per cent. Importantly, RBS had the controlling share because the business was to be written under their banking licence and on their balance sheet.

The Virgin Direct Group of companies then divided into three. The original Virgin Direct; Virgin Direct Money Managers; and Virgin One.

The plan was that Rowan would sit above all three companies, each of which would have its own Managing Director.

After a couple of false starts, Paul Pester, then an AMP employee, became Managing Director of Virgin Direct. Craig Meller took on the Money Managers. And I became responsible for building the Virgin One account from scratch. Because it was a bank, everything was different – products, regulations, partners. And I knew nothing about banking. So, the kitchen-table test became key. How could we make this technically complex product something that we could fully understand – and then make sure that customers could understand it, too?

We decided that the only way was to create a completely new and independent business. We rented more buildings on the same site as Discovery House, and took about eighty of the Virgin Direct team to build the new Virgin One account.

The division hurt everyone. We had all been so close. Those coming to Virgin One felt that they had been cut adrift from the mother ship. Those left behind felt that the others had sailed off with the family silver.

For those of us at Virgin One, it was another new beginning. As far as I could, I took the old, trusted team with me: Geoff, Ant, Kevin, Mark, Roland, and many of the brightest teleops and support teams.

But I needed people from RBS too, and didn't have so much control there. So Dave Dyer, who had brought the idea to us in the first place, joined the team. The only trouble was … I couldn't stand him. And the feeling was largely reciprocated. But he was clever and brought banking knowledge and an introduction to RBS.

Once again, my networking skills were going to be needed – this time in a big bank – if we were to pull this one off. And we also needed to bring new people into the team.

Back in Norwich Union days, when I had been an accountant, I worked for a wonderful man called Andrew Sage. He was probably the cleverest – and most down to earth – person I had ever met. And he had a unique smell about him, due to constantly trying to hide evidence of his crafty cigarettes with packets of extra-strong mints.

You could also tell the season by Andrew's appearance. When he decided that autumn had arrived, he would start wearing a jumper to work and grow a beard. We would know when he had decided that it was the first day of spring because he would arrive at work without either the jumper or the beard.

I was as pleased as punch to find that Andrew was prepared to leave NU and come and head up the Finance team as we built the One account. And I was surprised at how well he got on with Dave Dyer. Thank goodness.

Meanwhile, Ant had brought in a number of new business analysts to help us build the bank. One was a chemist who had subsequently worked at Arthur Andersen – Paul Lloyd. I always remember Paul telling me, as we built the One account, that while I would use it to maximise my borrowings, he would use it to pay off his debts as fast as possible – so that he could take off, unencumbered, whenever he wanted. Almost twenty years and three children later he is, thank goodness, well encumbered and still with us.

And we needed a Sales Director. To our surprise, Caroline Marsh, who had run the CEO's office under Martin Taylor at Barclays and subsequently headed up Sales at Barclays Premier, applied for the job.

We knew we had to be properly professional to attract her to Virgin One. But the day of her interview was the day of our 1998 Christmas party. Geoff was dressed as an elf. Ant was Father Christmas and had needed quite a bit of Dutch courage to get into the festive spirit. I had just given the Queen's Speech and was still wearing a tiara.

We all interviewed Caroline in our Christmas outfits. She didn't bat an eyelid. And to our surprise, she joined us. Almost twenty years later, she is also still with us. Thank goodness.

Meanwhile, the team were pointing out that Dave Dyer had actually proved to be a real find. He kept us on the straight and narrow, challenged me and was as passionate as the rest of us about what we were doing. He and Andrew Sage were doing a remarkable job in Finance and I could see that we really needed Dave to join us full time – not as the RBS representative on the partnership.

So, we set about trying to persuade Dave to join us. He was living in Edinburgh with his wife and two small girls and had never imagined moving down to Norwich. But he did. And almost twenty years later he is still with us. Thank goodness, yet again.

Building the Virgin One account was important for everyone involved. It made a difference to customers' lives. And every single member of the management team bought the product themselves with no persuasion at all. That said it all – it was a fabulous product.

It was another business that was built quickly. I always say that it went live in sixty-three days – from agreement to public launch – which it did. But the team point out that there was still much to do to provide the finished product.

We built the sales capability first, then servicing processes in the hope that there would be no difficult servicing challenges, divorces or deaths during the first few months. Then we built the annual review processes, which were not required for a year post launch. That way we always kept ahead of what our customers needed – but without slowing progress any more than necessary. It is a project technique that I continue to support.

One of our big achievements in that first sixty-three days was our introduction of daily interest calculations on mortgages.

I had not realised until that point that many banks at the time calculated mortgage interest monthly. Some even calculated it annually. That meant that customers were charged much more interest than they should have been because it was calculated on the outstanding balance at the beginning of the period – regardless of how much had been paid down in the meantime.

We thought that very unfair and it also spoilt the mathematical pureness of the One account. If customers were to get the benefit of putting their savings and current account balances against their loan balances, then it was essential that interest was calculated against the outstanding loan balance every day.

So we built a daily interest calculation. I believe we were one of the very first banks to do that. And now all mortgages calculate interest that way, saving every single mortgage customer in the UK a significant amount of money. Lots of people worked really hard to make this happen and should be proud to have made that important difference to UK mortgage customers over the ensuing years.

We wanted to help customers make the most of their account at all times and so Paul spent a huge amount of his time on the annual review process that showed customers how much they had spent and saved with their Virgin One account over the previous year. Paul concluded that we should help customers to make the most of the account by telling them how to minimise their balance every day. Even now, I meet people who were Virgin One account customers in those days and they still thank us for helping them to pay off their mortgage early.

Customers loved the approach. And although on a case-by-case basis we could certainly have made more money, it also brought us many more customers than we otherwise would have had. Doing the right thing proved to be the profitable thing every time.

We maintained our standard of having warm, friendly and knowledgeable people both selling and servicing the product, and that, combined with an emerging online presence, led to the most powerful marketing of all – happy and effusive customers telling their friends that the Virgin One account was a 'must have'.

Before long, we ran out of space on the business park, and found an office building on the other side of the city. Woodland Place could seat around 300 staff, but before long we had run out of room there, too, and had people (including me and my team) working in stacked Portakabins in the car park.

We managed to lease the building next door, a newspaper warehouse that had location in its favour and very little else, and converted it into an inspiring building to work in with lots of natural light, a mezzanine floor and a huge canteen.

We had a lot of fun along the way. Roland would have fancy-dress days for the call-centre team from time to time. Imagine my surprise one day when two armed police units turned into our car park at Woodland Place because they had received reports of two men dressed as cowboys and carrying rifles at the local petrol station. They were toys, of course, but we didn't do that again.

But business was good, to the surprise of the detractors. Even Gordon McCallum, on my Board to represent the Virgin Group, had announced that he thought we would do well ever to sell 10,000 One accounts in a year.

In the first year we sold 2,011. I remember it well as Ant promised to dye his black hair peroxide blond if we exceeded our target of 2,000. And we did. And he did.

The next year, we sold 18,750 accounts. The word-of-mouth advertising, together with some great TV ads, had helped to create some real momentum.

At our peak, we had built the business to £25 billion of outstanding facilities and had turned the One account quickly to profit – despite helping people to minimise their debt and to pay it off fast. Customers were prepared to pay a higher rate for that, for excellent service and for the financial flexibility that the account provided.

RBS were delighted with the success of the product and I joined the Board of their Retail Direct division run by Norman McLuskie.

But, in the meantime, much was changing – both for RBS and for Virgin.

One day, Dave and I were in London, in a taxi, passing the big redbrick building on Holborn which, at the time, was home to the RBS London offices. 'I see RBS have appointed Fred Goodwin to take over from George Mathewson,' said Dave. 'That's interesting. I remember Fred turned down the CFO job when he was offered it.'

We both reflected on this news, wondering how it might impact us.

And impact us it did.

Not long after, and before he had taken over from George as CEO, Fred came to see us in Norwich. Dave and I met him in my office.

'This product will never work the way you've set it up,' said Fred.

'Says who?' said Dave, in his normal accommodating style.

'Says me,' said Fred, glaring. Our cards were marked from then on.

Soon after, Fred took over as CEO, and soon after that, he and George embarked on the deal to buy NatWest bank. Norman was left to run RBS while the deal was being done.

I enjoyed being on the periphery of that – flying up to Scotland once or twice a month for Norman's divisional Board and hearing the real story behind what I was reading in the papers every day. But I also enjoyed being able to escape and focus on my own business with just enough contact, but no unnecessary interference, from my RBS colleagues, who had so much else on their plates.

As the One account grew, things were more difficult back at Virgin Direct. Rowan, always ahead of his time, was very keen to take advantage of the internet. He could see clearly the potential of the online lifestyles that the world has now adopted. He was pushing hard to turn Virgin Direct into an online-only business.

But AMP had other ideas, and at the same time they were facing problems of their own – both back home in Australia, and with the Pearl Assurance business in the UK. Virgin Direct needed more money to expand and to support Rowan's vision, but AMP were not prepared to increase their investment. And that was holding back the flourishing Virgin One account too.

RBS were becoming alarmed that their partner in the One account business was becoming dysfunctional.

I remember clearly at this time going to see Richard Branson in his Holland Park house and meeting the CEO of AMP – Paul Batchelor. Richard was hopeful of compromising with AMP so all the businesses could move forward. But Paul remained resolute.

After he left, Richard sighed deeply and put his head in his hands.

'What do you really want out of all this?' I asked him.

'The same as I always want,' he said. 'If we can see an opportunity where customers are badly served then I want Virgin to serve them better.'

I have always looked for those opportunities ever since.

After that it was clear that the only people who could unlock the stalemate were RBS. I called Norman and told him about the situation and my concerns. He was hugely supportive and said that RBS would do all they could to help.

Not long after the NatWest deal was signed, Norman invited me and Richard Branson to meet with him and Fred Goodwin at the Orangery in Holland Park to discuss what might be done.

Being in the company of three very important people, I had already decided not to have a drink, but during the course of the evening the others downed a bottle or two of expensive white wine.

We talked about the NatWest deal and how Fred had pulled it off. And it was agreed that RBS would make an offer to Virgin Direct to acquire 100 per cent of the Virgin One account. We were to be a full subsidiary of one of the biggest banks in the world.

Everyone shook hands and Fred and Norman left me and Richard to celebrate.

'You haven't had a drink,' he said. 'Let's have another bottle of that delicious white wine.'

When we had finished he patted his pockets. 'Have you got any money on you?' asked Richard. 'I seem to have left mine behind.'

And that's how I ended up paying for expensive wine for Norman, Richard Branson and Fred Goodwin.

Chapter 4

LIFE AT RBS

2000–2007

'We know PPI is a problem. But we can't be the first bank to stop it. It will decimate the share price.'

Losing Our Virginity

AFTER THE meeting with Richard, Fred and Norman, work began on the deal, and in October 2001 RBS became 100 per cent owners of the Virgin One account and of all the people that went with it. The whole business was valued at £130 million and everyone was very happy with that.

On the day the deal was signed, I received a handwritten letter from Richard Branson.

'Congratulations!' it said. 'But I feel a bit bad that I've sold you and the team along with the rest of the business. If ever you get fed up with corporate life then call me and you can come back.'

I was pleased to get that assurance, but very excited about a new life with RBS. It simply never crossed my mind that the letter would become very important indeed.

To start with, very little changed when we became fully employed by RBS. The business stayed in Norwich and so did the team. I travelled backwards and forwards more often to Edinburgh and was fully involved in all of the RBS executive management sessions, but my focus remained the Virgin One account, which continued to flourish – so much so that we built RBS- and NatWest-branded One accounts too.

In December that year, Ash and I were away for a weekend in France when I discovered that I was pregnant.

I had suffered several miscarriages and five failed IVF attempts over recent years and we had almost given up hope of having a baby.

But on the sixth IVF attempt I fell pregnant, at the age of forty.

I was thrilled and terrified at the same time and concluded that having a baby would not change my life at all. We would find a way of making it fit in.

That year was hard work and I worked through to 12 August 2002 – just two weeks before my baby was due.

True to form – I hate lateness in any circumstances – Amy arrived on her due date of 25 August and I was bowled over with love – so much so that I just couldn't imagine going back to work. Ever.

I had told Norman that I would be back six weeks after the birth. Fortunately, Norman had appointed one of his team, Philippa Dickson, to take charge of running the business in my absence, perhaps not trusting my optimism completely. Just as well, as I was hit with a truly astonishing bout of post-natal depression.

I had never really understood depression before – thinking it a sign of weakness. But the dark moments of despair were real, physical and frightening. I refused to have any medication, having seen my mother struggle to wean herself off anti-depressants over a number of years. I just pushed through regardless and went back to work.

I had to. I was the sole breadwinner – Ash had given up work to look after the baby – and so there was no choice.

By January 2003 I was back at work but I knew I had to find a way to give up both for my health and for my baby. So I determined to get a bit of balance back for a bit: to do my job well but not get in too early and never work later than 6 p.m.

At the end of the year I went to see Norman to discuss my performance. And, to my surprise, I was awarded my best-ever bonus.

'How can that be?' I asked. 'I've worked fewer hours and things have been less intense.'

'I suspect,' said Norman, 'that now you have something that's more important to you than work, it is giving you a better perspective. You've had a great year.'

Meanwhile, I was certainly finding out more about how a big bank worked, and how the people who worked within it thought and behaved.

Every year, Fred Goodwin used to take all the executive team up to Gleneagles for an annual review and general team building. One year, there were pre-dinner drinks in the Glendevon room and I was speaking with Fred about his journey to becoming CEO of RBS.

He had run Clydesdale Bank, which was then owned by National Australia Bank, and had been posted to Melbourne into a bigger group job. One day he got a call from George Mathewson asking him to come back to Scotland as CFO of RBS.

'I told him to call again when he wanted me to replace him as CEO,' said Fred.

So, some time later, Fred returned one night to his Melbourne office and saw a yellow Post-it on his desk. The note from his

PA said, 'Please call George Mathewson.' And Fred knew that the time had come for him to return to Scotland as CEO of RBS.

As he told me the story, that night in Gleneagles, he reached inside his jacket pocket, took out his wallet and showed me – all those years later – that yellow Post-it note. And I realised then how much the role mattered to him.

Following Amy's arrival, I had been reflecting on what mattered to me, too.

Not long after her birth, I had a meeting in the Sprowston Manor hotel in Norwich with a large number of the Virgin One account team. We were there to talk about a new marketing campaign, but I found myself opening up about being a new mum.

I remember saying that I no longer wanted to come to work just to do my job but that the only way it made sense for me to leave my child was to do something meaningful – something that would make a bit of a positive difference in the world.

I had no idea what I really meant by that. But, to my surprise, when I looked up, people were in tears. So many men and women had empathy with my own struggle to prioritise between the importance of my daughter and that of my job. And I realised then that no one in that room got out of bed in the morning just to answer the telephone, fill in an application form or send out bank statements. Most of us want to make a difference.

I wanted to find a way for all of the people in that room to feel as if they could make a difference by coming to work – a difference to their own and their family's wellbeing, of course, but beyond that, a difference to their community, however that was defined. These were grand thoughts and hard to express outside my immediate team, never mind in the more corporate world that RBS was becoming.

Making It Happen

Meanwhile, RBS continued to flourish and grow – so much so that a decision was made to build a new head office in Edinburgh, inspired, I believe, by the Santander HQ in Madrid. Santander's Emilio Botín had been a good personal and professional friend to Fred Goodwin and George Mathewson, and had provided them with critical and unswerving support on the NatWest deal.

I remember sitting in Norman's office in St Andrew Square in Edinburgh as the first soil was turned to build the new RBS head office in Gogarburn.

'I hope it's going to be okay,' said Norman. 'You hear time and time again that when an organisation is confident enough to indulge in big head offices, that's the time that the rot sets in.' We all laughed. But I never forgot it.

In 2004 Norman announced that he planned to retire, and all of my Retail Direct colleagues were keen to find out who their new boss would be. Soon, Fred announced that Chris Sullivan would be appointed to run Retail Direct, and to be a member of Fred's executive team.

Chris was an unknown quantity to the Retail Direct team. He had worked at NatWest all his life and had been instrumental in the success of Lombard – as well as Angel Trains after it had been taken over by RBS in 1997. To my surprise, when I first met him in his office he had a model of a Virgin train on display.

Chris was very much a family man – with seven children to prove it. And he wanted a strong cohesive team to run Retail Direct and take it from strength to strength.

In 2004 he asked me to move from Norwich to Edinburgh to become a full part of the Scottish team and to run the Lombard and Direct Line financial services brands – as well as the Virgin One account.

It was an easy decision for me and Ash. It meant less travelling for me and a new start in an exciting new city, and we felt it would help us to spend more time together with two-year-old Amy and to get a better work–life balance as a family.

The only problem for me was leaving my mum and dad behind in Norfolk. As an only child myself and having my own only child so late in life, my parents absolutely loved Amy and we were all very close.

As a result, as Ash and I were house hunting, we looked for a house big enough to accommodate all five of us – three generations – and with enough space to ensure that we didn't get under each other's feet. We found such a house near Morningside in Edinburgh and Ash, Amy and I moved up in June 2005.

My first day in my expanded role was the first day that the new RBS Gogarburn office complex was open for business.

It was an amazing place. A long street with Tesco on the right, followed by a hairdresser and Starbucks. You could sit and have a meeting in the street while having your coffee. The office space went off the street in 'wings' and at the very end of the street was the executive block, which was well guarded and sparsely populated by Fred and only his most senior executives – including Chris.

That wing also included the 'mess', which was where executives could have lunch together. The idea was to make sure that executives had an opportunity to meet up over lunch and to communicate with each other. It felt a good thing to be 'in'. But it wasn't great to be 'out'.

Christmas lunches there were reportedly long affairs. I never went. But I know they went on well into the night, reputedly with the smoke alarms switched off so that cigars could be enjoyed.

There were also dinners – again which I never attended – where the after-dinner entertainment included dipping a thumb in sambuca, setting it alight, and passing the flame, thumb to thumb, around the table, seeing who would keep the flame alight the longest. A number of senior executives had burns the next day and I suspect some still carry the scars.

Rumour had it that, after the success of the NatWest deal, a dinner was held in the old 'mess' in St Andrew Square and, after dinner, the sambuca game commenced. One of the women bankers who had been on the deal did not want her thumb set alight – but her boss insisted she should do it. So she did to save embarrassment.

I did go to a few events, and I recall one evening in the St Andrew Square mess when everyone had been asked to come with a party piece. One senior executive was missing as he was overseas, in China. RBS was in the throes of expanding into the Far East, eventually paying £1.6 billion for a 10 per cent stake in the Bank of China. Fred asked what the missing party piece was to have been and we learned that the executive had planned to impersonate Elvis.

A conference phone was brought in, and the executive was called. It was the middle of the night in China and he was in bed.

'It's Fred Goodwin here. I'm calling to ask you to do your Elvis impersonation.'

And after only a brief moment's hesitation, down the phone line came 'Well it's a-one for the money ... '

All of this was designed to be fun, I am sure, and a way of building the team – but it did leave me feeling some discomfort. There were very few women involved and the peer pressure to be part of this world was very real. And if you were not on the inside of this cliquey behaviour, then you could end up suspicious and resentful of those who were.

Worse, however, seemed to be happening in the HR department. I had been oblivious to the issues there until one night at a Gleneagles executive event when a female friend of mine, who was a senior member of staff in her own right, bemoaned the fact that it was expected that she would spend the night with her manager.

I was truly astounded. But I know that was not an isolated event.

At the same time, inside RBS, politics seemed to be taking hold in a way I had not really seen before.

Fred was very focused on new acquisitions, and the Retail businesses seemed to be less important now that NatWest had been fully and successfully integrated into RBS.

That had been an amazing deal, which demonstrated all of Fred's capabilities and which impressed and inspired people within and without the organisation. As a deal and as a project it could not have gone better. That was down to teamwork, a good plan, absolute and resolute determination to hit targets, and a real view within the business that it was a brilliant opportunity to prove that a relatively small Scottish bank could first take over an English bank – and then become one of the biggest banks in the world.

As Fred (or Sir Fred, as he became in 2004) focused on building global scale and reach, Gordon Pell took over the Retail business and Retail Direct was integrated into Gordon's organisation, with Chris becoming Gordon's second-in-command.

I joined Gordon's top team, having been asked to run RBS's UK mortgage business – of which the One account had become a not insignificant part – and, as always, the brilliant people from the Virgin days came with me, including, among others, Caroline, Dave and Paul. Along the way, of course, we had met other great people who extended our team and expanded our knowledge.

But it still seemed to me that the kitchen-table test was important – and I remained a big fan of asking the stupid question. When we took over managing the Lombard loans business, I just couldn't see how the accounting was working properly, and I feared that we may be overstating profits.

As a team, we sat down for hours in the posh meeting rooms in Gogarburn – often provided, I remember, with meat pies – and tried to understand how the loan accounting matched our understanding of the business. And the fact was that it did not.

We tried to engage with the central finance team – the ones who patrolled accounting policies, made journal entries and who were responsible for the numbers reported to the market – and for a very long time they just would not agree that anything was wrong.

Then we looked at the accounting for Direct Line loans. It was done in the same way and they had made the same error.

. Together the errors were many millions of pounds in this one year alone. We could hardly bring ourselves to think how many years it had been going on for.

In the end the central accountants agreed. We had a big problem. And as I had found it, I had the challenge of going to Fred to tell him. I was not looking forward to this. Fred was a notoriously difficult recipient of bad news. As predicted, he was furious, and he did, straight off, shoot the messenger.

'That cannot be right,' he snapped. 'If you're right, then the cost to RBS and NatWest businesses will be huge.' And so it was.

Not to be deterred, we determined to sell more to make up for the financial hole that we had found. However, in trying to do so, we came across a further issue that I found even more uncomfortable. It soon became very clear indeed that unsecured loans were being priced in such a way that profit was only being made on them through the sale of credit insurance – otherwise known as payment-protection insurance (PPI).

Unsecured loans were extremely competitive, and the cheaper the loan, the better credit quality the banks were able to attract. So, to fight for the best customers, banks pushed loan rates lower and lower until they were unprofitable.

In order to return a profit, it became an accepted practice to add on a product to the loan that would actually make money. Unsecured loan customers could lose their jobs, so it made sense to offer them insurance to protect their incomes if they became unemployed. This was the now infamous PPI.

The trouble was that when customers wanted a loan many thought that the PPI was something they had to have in order to be approved for it. And the sales process did little to disabuse them of this thought.

As Caroline and I tried to manage the call centres – in Tannochside and Rotherham – which sold this business and the attached PPI, we could see what a problem this could be.

I went to see one of the senior executives to seek his advice.

'I really think we are storing up a problem with PPI, and I think we should stop it,' I said.

'We know PPI is a problem,' he replied. 'But we can't be the first bank to stop it. It will damage the share price.'

Project Stone

Around about this time, RBS looked at acquiring Northern Rock.

Northern Rock was a flourishing mortgage business and a darling of the City. In addition to being seen as innovative and dynamic, it was pretty ambitious – the 2005 annual results showed record profits of £308 million, an increase of 14 per cent on the previous year. Lending had also grown materially.

Despite every effort – on paper at least – an acquisition was ruled out because the business was protected by the nicest of poisoned pills – the Northern Rock Foundation. Any purchaser would have to pay a premium to this excellent north-east charity on acquisition and it meant that the economics just did not stack up for any potential buyer – including RBS.

But it seemed that Northern Rock was doing something right. A measure of efficiency in any business is the cost–income ratio (in other words how much it costs to generate a pound of income) and Northern Rock's cost–income ratio was one of the lowest in the sector. It was telling that, in 2005, RBS's cost–income ratio had fallen to 46.1 per cent after a lot of hard work to drive it below 50 per cent. In the same year, Northern Rock's figure was 30.2 per cent.

Northern Rock's growth was largely driven by a huge share of mortgages – it charged very low rates on traditional lending and remortgages – and through an innovative new 'Together' account that allowed customers to borrow up to 125 per cent of the value of their home.

Together account customers could borrow almost six times their income, sometimes with no deposit. The first 95 per cent of the loan was secured as a mortgage and there was up to 30 per cent more available as a personal loan. Great for first-time buyers or those making a fresh start, but every customer suffered negative equity until their property had increased in value materially.

Northern Rock also boasted arrears and credit losses that were the lowest in the market. They charged low prices on unsecured lending – and topped up their profits with PPI.

As the person responsible for the RBS mortgage business, Gordon was starting to ask me why we were not achieving the same results as Northern Rock. Dave and I scratched our heads – we simply could not see how we could match what Northern Rock was achieving.

We simply could not match their pricing and their products and make money within our own risk appetite. I started to doubt myself; clearly my competence to grow the business was starting to come under close scrutiny.

To make matters worse, other banks were making lots of money by securitising high volumes of mortgages and we simply could not get to a place where we could see how that could be done safely.

But I was told that, at morning meetings with Fred, the Investment division was asking Gordon Pell why RBS was missing out on such a lucrative profit stream, and Gordon expected me to sort it out. As a result, Gordon initiated a project called Project Stone. The aim was to consider introducing RBS to the world of mortgage securitisation.

Dave and I made several journeys down to the RBS investment bank at Bishopsgate in London to try to understand how we might make this happen. But we could never see how it made sense.

Of course, this all sounds great with hindsight – as if Dave and I saw the crisis coming. The truth is that we did not. The simple truth – the kitchen-table test if you like – was that we felt stupid. It seemed as if the real bankers were cleverer than us and could find ways of doing business that we simply could not understand.

In September 2005 the Queen visited RBS Gogarburn to open the new offices. It was a huge honour, and the place and people were ship-shape for the royal visit, which included a fly-past by four RAF Tornadoes.

Caroline and I were chosen to meet the Queen and Prince Philip and we were introduced to them by George and Fred respectively. It struck us how well briefed they were – and how well orchestrated the visit was – but that the Duke of Edinburgh was determined to go 'off-piste' and talk to people that had not been pre-rehearsed. And boy, had we been pre-rehearsed! Clearly, our royal visitors knew how organisations work and that the real people often know what is going on much better than those at the top.

The royal visit cemented the success of RBS in our minds, and our inability to get to grips with Project Stone made us feel even less capable. One afternoon, I went to present our findings to Fred and Gordon and to recommend that we should not securitise mortgages.

Fred immediately agreed. To my genuine surprise, he thought the whole thing was a sham. But Gordon was not so sure. The next day he asked another member of the Retail Division to take over Project Stone and to try again.

Some years later, I spoke to one of the Risk Directors who had been at RBS during that time and asked him what had happened to Project Stone. 'I think the recommendation continued to be not to do it,' he said, 'but the Investment Division did it anyway.'

At the same time as I was feeling uncomfortable about my own capability, RBS was going into the strategic planning cycle for the year ahead. It was August 2006 and the initial financial plans needed to be produced in September.

Dave and I did our best to push the mortgage plans to achieve good results, but margins were coming down, Northern Rock was taking material market share, and, of course, we did not securitise mortgages. As a result, our budgeted profit for the mortgage division in 2007 was lower than in 2006.

Gordon and the accountants made it clear to me and to Dave that this was simply not acceptable.

As we walked together along one of the upstairs corridors in RBS Gogarburn, looking down on the street, and weighed down with misery, I very clearly remember saying to Dave, 'I just don't get this. If they're not careful, RBS will end up the next Enron' (the American energy company had gone bankrupt five years earlier).

It never occurred to us, though, that anything was fundamentally wrong with the business – just that it was being pushed too hard, partly by the markets, which expected double-digit improvements in profitability year after year. There was nothing that implied any lack of integrity – Fred would never have stood for that – and nothing that seemed a regulatory concern, but, taken together, the many pressures to perform and to deliver in the face of an extreme competitive environment became unsustainable.

So much has been written about RBS since the financial crisis that it has become more of a story than a reality. But my experiences there were very real and I knew everyone involved – on the UK side at least.

I have been saddened by the fall of Fred Goodwin. He was a brilliant man who focused on driving shareholder value and excellent customer service. I have reflected long and hard on how the exact opposite has been achieved. In my opinion there were at least four big reasons for RBS's downfall in 2008.

Firstly, the bank grew too big, too fast, and, as a result, management lost control. The genuine success of the NatWest acquisition created an environment where the senior team thought they just could not fail. Fred was named the best CEO in the world by *Fortune* magazine, and that edition was put in every bedroom at the executive conference that year. Surely the lesson is never to believe such publicity.

Secondly, the growth was built on foundations of sand. There simply was not enough capital to support such rapid asset growth. In my experience, there was little consideration of capital at all, especially in a world where continued economic prosperity was largely taken for granted. I remember being in a meeting with Fred when he questioned why we needed mortgage valuations for all properties that we lent against.

'There's no need,' he said. 'Property prices are only going one way in the UK. And that's up.'

His confidence was genuine, compelling but, as it turned out, misguided. There is no doubt in my mind that the capital requirements and stress-testing regime that have been introduced post crisis are necessary and right.

Thirdly, RBS suffered from a complete lack of diversity at the top of the organisation. The vast majority of the senior team were white, Scottish men. Joining RBS was the first and only time that I, personally, have experienced what racism must feel like. I was welcomed into the bank and invited to dinners and parties, so I never felt excluded, but I definitely felt English. Sometimes, especially after rugby matches, being English didn't feel great. It was subtle, but real.

In 2009 I asked Sir Brian Pitman, who had previously been Chairman of Lloyds, if he had considered becoming Chairman of RBS to lead it out of crisis.

'I wouldn't do that,' he said. 'It's full of Scottish interests. It would be impossible to get anything done.'

I was surprised at his reaction. I hadn't really noticed before. But, as always, Sir Brian was right. At the very least, RBS was run by a bunch of like-minded men with similar educational backgrounds, and at the time no one saw the problems that created.

It is the reason that diversity on boards, in business and in teams seems to me an important part of running good and safe organisations in the future.

Finally, the growth, success and celebration of RBS created an unhealthy environment where many senior managers really did think that they were Masters of the Universe. That led to a change in ethics in the business, and that is when I knew it was time to go. Employees throughout the business were aware that at least one director would turn up for work the worse for wear on several mornings, and rumours of affairs were rife. When, a year or so later, a journalist rang me and asked, 'What can you tell me about senior managers having affairs at RBS?', I realised that many more answers went through my head than I would have liked or expected (and of course, I told the journalist nothing).

I don't want to sound prudish, but I do think that our business leaders need to be beyond reproach if they are to lead many thousands of people to provide a trusted service to customers whose money they look after. Culture is important in banking, as we have seen since the crisis, and, in my view, regulators are right to monitor it and to expect it to be good.

I have learned over the years that extraordinary success tends to suggest unusual behaviours. Those salespeople who outperform the norm should be checked out. Banks which claim to be beating the market when they represent material market share are probably fooling themselves and others. Masters of the Universe are probably not all they believe themselves to be.

Hubris is best avoided by surrounding yourself with people who keep your feet on the ground. Thank goodness for Dave Dyer.

The Great Escape

One Thursday morning in October 2006, Dave and Paul came into my office in Gogarburn.

'We can't go on like this,' they said. 'Do you remember, when we sold the One account, that Richard said we could go back if we hated corporate life? Well, now's the time to do it. Pick up the phone and call him.'

And, despite the fact that I had not spoken to Richard or the Virgin team for a year or two, that is exactly what I did.

It was Gordon McCallum whom I called on that morning, from my office, with Dave and Paul hanging on my every word.

I don't even recall many niceties in our conversation before I said to Gordon, 'Do you remember Richard said we could come back if we fell out of love with corporate life? Well, we're ready to come back now.'

To my surprise, and without a moment's hesitation, Gordon said, 'The timing could be perfect. Can you come down to London on Tuesday?'

So, off I went to meet Gordon the following Tuesday, first in his townhouse in Chelsea and then in the local deli, where we had brunch. It all felt very sophisticated.

I told Gordon about our issues with RBS – but we talked more about our plans to rebuild the Virgin One account back on home territory, and to try and take on the apparent success of Northern Rock.

He told me that, in parallel with our own trials and tribulations at RBS, things had been tough at Virgin Direct.

It was now renamed Virgin Money. There had been some innovative product development. It had spent heavily developing its online capability, and had branched out into Australia and South Africa. But in the UK the income from its insurance and investment business was insufficient to cover costs – even with a new credit-card partnership with MBNA.

As a result, there had been a succession of management changes. Rowan had left to set up Virgin Wines and Paul Pester had joined Santander. As a result, the business was being run by someone new to me – Mark Hodgkinson – who was very able, but who came from a process and operational background rather than a commercial one. The business model had been to outsource as much of the direct operation as possible, although there were still around 200 people working in the business. More significantly, the tensions with AMP had come to a head and Richard Branson had bought them out of the business and now owned the whole thing outright.

All of this meant that the Virgin Group were considering the future of their 100-per-cent-owned financial services business at the very moment that my call came in.

It didn't take long to agree that I would return to Virgin Money. Two days later, Richard called to welcome me back and I started to plan both my escape from RBS and reappearance at Virgin Money.

I resigned immediately from RBS. Given all the disagreements, there was really not much surprise, although I did get a warm and supportive letter from Fred.

When I showed it to my mother she said, 'I really cannot understand why you are leaving a blue-chip company like RBS and joining a tiny company like Virgin Money. What's got into you?'

It shook me, as she was otherwise so supportive. But it was done now and there was no choice but to make it work.

The question was how to spring the rest of the team. As well as Dave and Paul, Caroline, Roland, Kevin and many others were chomping at the bit to get out of RBS and back to Virgin, too. Over the next six months, over eighty people moved back to Virgin Money. A risk for everyone, and one that weighed heavily on me, affecting as it did the livelihood of so many families.

At the other end of the spectrum were the existing Virgin Money team, who needed to be looked after and to buy in to the new direction.

But as I was on garden leave from RBS at the time and unable to say where I was going, we had to plan the next steps carefully. Despite the difficulties of being in the limbo of garden leave, it felt ridiculously good to be back at Virgin. The culture was even further away from that of RBS than I had remembered.

There was an exciting buzz and an atmosphere of youthful innovation. More importantly still, Richard had taken himself out of the day-to-day running of the businesses and decision making had become completely decentralised. So, each business was free to make its own decisions without any central bureaucracy or unnecessary control.

The controlling factor was the brand and what it stood for. As long as every business lived up to the brand values, and as long as everything each business did positively enhanced them, then broadly everything else fell into place. Much like starting the Virgin Direct business, there was no blueprint; we just asked ourselves what a financial services business with the Virgin brand ought to look and feel like.

Of course, every business had to have its own governance and controls – but that was the responsibility of each CEO and their Board. That was about as far away from my RBS experience as you could get.

The last thing I did before leaving RBS was to present to Fred a new mortgage process to increase branch sales. It did not go well. We did it in the main Birmingham branch of NatWest, and as soon as I saw that the local branch manager was sporting a Mohican hair style I knew we would struggle.

After that session, Caroline and I had agreed to meet a new member of the Virgin Group – Matt Baxby – an Australian, whom Gordon suggested should join our team once we were back at Virgin. We met on a Birmingham New Street station platform and immediately hit it off. Both Matt and his brother David had enjoyed impressive careers in the Virgin Group – David for Virgin's airline interests in Asia Pacific, while Matt had left a successful legal career in Brisbane to come to London in 2003 as an investment advisor to the Virgin Group.

At about the same time, Dave resigned from RBS – a big decision for him with two teenage girls to support. RBS were unsurprised, as we had worked together for years, and once I had left, Craig Donaldson, who took over from me, wanted to bring in finance people of his own. Dave was put on garden leave, too.

For me, garden leave was great. Amy was just over four years old, and I valued the time with her hugely, and Ash and I decided to go on a big trip while I had the time.

So we booked to go to Ulusaba – Richard Branson's game reserve in the Kruger National Park in South Africa. Richard had bought two farms there at the suggestion of Nelson Mandela, and they were stunningly beautiful.

We flew on Virgin Atlantic and I realised again, thinking about the logistics of running a huge airline, just how astonishing all of Richard's achievements had been.

But that was really the only break. The rest of my garden leave was spent planning for my return when it was finally public. And that meant a lot of worrying about how to set up the One account anew.

There was a general view in the Virgin Group that we would all move to London. I lay in bed in Edinburgh at night fretting about that. I knew people in Norwich. I knew people in Edinburgh. Good people who could build a business and run a bank. But I did not know those sort of people in London.

I rang Gordon and said I thought we should rebuild Virgin Money from Edinburgh and Norwich. He sounded very dubious.

But two days later he rang back. 'Richard's keen that you stay in Edinburgh,' he said. 'He says that people are always most successful when they are happiest. So over to you.'

Great news. And more pressure!

Other than Dave and myself, we had no one yet on the team in Edinburgh. But Matt agreed immediately to move up with his wife and baby daughter. They rented a lovely house and arrived within a week. The Virgin way – once a decision is made, you get on with it.

And so we turned my house – and especially the dining room – into the Virgin Money HQ. Dave, Matt and I worked out of there every day, and as new people joined us the house got busier. There were always piles of shoes at the door and Ash became expert at making copious cups of tea.

We spent our time planning how to rebuild the One account, how to make the loss-making business profitable, and how to market it most effectively.

Over the years, I had worked with Johnny Hornby and always loved his creativity and energy as he set up his own ad agency and helped the businesses I ran – both at the original Virgin One account and at RBS.

Johnny had worked at famous advertising agencies such as Ogilvy & Mather, CDP and TBWA, where he was in charge of advertising for the Labour Party's successful 2001 general election campaign. He had launched a new agency, CHI, with two industry friends, which had gone from strength to strength, and had maintained his warmth and integrity throughout. I trusted him completely.

So we brought Johnny into our confidence and asked him up to Edinburgh one day to meet me, Dave and Matt.

The challenge was to find a marketing campaign that would make sense of the broad product range at Virgin Money. As things were, credit cards, insurance and investments were all marketed separately and there was nothing to link them sensibly together. Add a mortgage like the One account and we all knew that customers would be confused about what Virgin Money was and, importantly, what we stood for.

Because we had all taken such a risk – financially, personally and professionally – in leaving RBS, we realised that our aspirations for the business and for ourselves were beyond the drive for profits that had motivated us to leave RBS. We wanted to do more and to achieve something more purposeful if we could.

Led by Johnny, we realised that one of the things we had hated at RBS was the 'win at all costs' culture.

Just before I left, I had been part of a team that role-played how RBS should react to a big cyber-attack by an overseas power. Part of the challenge was that the solution to the attack was to address an abuse of human rights in the other country. Almost everyone on the team concluded that it was more important to notify our government about the human rights breach than to resolve the specific RBS exposure.

Fred disagreed, saying that it was not the role of business to intervene in such matters – the role of business was solely to make money for shareholders.

I was not alone in struggling with that moral dilemma, but there was no such problem at Virgin. Richard had always been clear that he saw business as a source for good, and his leadership of the Elders programme – the group of global figures committed to peace and human rights – paid testimony to that.

We had celebrated Richard's fiftieth birthday with him at the One account and he was by now heading towards his sixtieth. His role in the Virgin empire had changed, and he had spent a great deal of time reflecting on what he could give back to society.

A few of us, in my Edinburgh dining room, thought about the purpose of Virgin Money, and agreed that we wanted to create a business that would do some good in the world, as well as making money for shareholders.

We had also seen some HR issues at RBS that we did not like. Just before I left, an anonymous letter had been sent to Fred about a junior member of my team. The letter writer thought that the employee was living beyond his means and therefore must be stealing from the business.

It turned out that the employee's father had died recently and had left him some money, but, in getting to that place of understanding, the RBS HR machine had assumed he was guilty before being proven innocent.

I was horrified at the way it was handled and my HR business partner, Matt Elliott, resigned because of the way he saw this individual being treated.

So we also decided that we wanted to make sure that all staff at Virgin Money were treated properly and had the opportunity to achieve their personal ambitions – be that to come to work to pay their mortgage ... or to come to work to change the world.

We also realised that the only way we could make real progress would be through building strong, win–win partnerships with as many people and organisations as possible.

At RBS there was a distrust that bordered on hatred of mortgage intermediaries. Fred and many of his team felt that they were an unnecessary mouth to feed for an organisation with a branch network as extensive as that belonging to RBS.

I disagreed and worked hard at building relationships with the leaders of all the big intermediary firms. They were all keen to work together to achieve the right outcome for our mutual customers, and I learned once again that if you work openly with other people you more often than not reap significant rewards together.

And focusing on the customer was, of course, at the heart of the Virgin brand – and always will be. Virgin is nothing if not a consumer champion fighting as far as possible for the best outcome for customers in everything we do.

As we discussed these points that day in Edinburgh, we realised that, as a team, our new business needed to address all of these points and that they were all equally important to us.

We concluded that we wanted to come up with a strategy and a business that would be more than a marketing campaign. It would be our driving force and our corporate ambition.

We wanted to make profit for our shareholders, of course – but not at the expense of the other key components of our working environment. We wanted our customers to love us. Our staff to realise their personal ambitions. Our communities to flourish. To build win–win deals with our partners. And, as a result, to earn good returns for our shareholders.

In short, we agreed that our ambition and purpose would be to make everyone better off.

Chapter 5

BUILDING A BANK

2007–2010

'I feel a bit bad that I've sold you and the team along with the rest of the business. If ever you get fed up with corporate life, then call me and you can come back.'

Back to the Future

WHILE WE were on garden leave, we were able to plan for the new One account and for a business that made everyone better off, but we couldn't get under the skin of Virgin Money until May 2007 – when I was released by RBS and the existing Virgin Money team could be told of the future plans for the business.

We were surprised at how well they took the news. Mark Hodgkinson left with a redundancy payment and with new job plans. Others stayed for a while but soon found new roles in other businesses.

It was not long before we found out why almost everyone in the old team was quite happy to go. The losses in the business were bigger than we had thought, and Dave and I found we had left RBS to join a company with negative reserves of £40 million and an owner who, as 2007 progressed, was needed to support the running of a large airline that was beginning to have challenges of its own.

In short, there was no money for us.

There were three obvious things we could try to do about it.

First, we hedged our FTSE exposure to protect future income. Hedging, in this context, meant that we were effectively taking out an insurance against market volatility, so that we'd reduce the impact of a fall in the market. Stock market ups and downs had been a real problem every year before that but we managed to lock down good deals year after year – sometimes as much by luck as by good judgement.

Next, we took a long hard look at the credit-card partnership that Paul Pester had agreed with MBNA in Chester. The business was doing well and volumes were good, but Virgin Money was getting only a commission payment for each sale, and that just was not a fair share of the economics, especially when we needed money to ensure our very survival.

On my first trip to Chester to meet the team there, Pete Ball and Dave Pemberton were full of a positive outlook, but with warnings about the state of the current relationship. The partnership, for a number of reasons, had reached a point of an unhealthy stand-off, and corporate and personal relationships were strained.

I remembered that time at Norwich Union when I had to face up to the regulators in an equally frosty situation, and how asking them for help had unlocked the problem.

So I did the same at MBNA.

I explained to the then Managing Director, Michael Rhodes, that the Virgin Money businesses needed a fairer share of the deal to survive, that we had a new way of addressing the market by making everyone better off and that we would move heaven and earth to start this relationship afresh and to make it work.

Michael agreed to look at everything again, and within a few weeks we had agreed a new contract, which gave us a partial profit share as well as commission for each card sold.

But there was one big problem. The Virgin Money credit-card partnership with MBNA relied on PPI to boost its profits. Having seen the problems that PPI was storing up (it is estimated that by May 2008 there were 20 million PPI policies in place in the UK, many of which would be subsequently classified as having been mis-sold), I was determined that we would not sell it at Virgin Money.

We had a meeting at the MBNA offices in Jermyn Street in London, where I told the MBNA team that I was not prepared to sell PPI on Virgin products.

They were flabbergasted, as they knew we needed the money. And they certainly were not prepared to lose profit for their own business in this way.

In the end, we agreed that MBNA could approach Virgin Money customers after the credit card had been sold, to see if PPI was right for them. It was sold by MBNA people under the MBNA brand. That way customers never felt they had to buy PPI to be approved for the Virgin Money credit card that they needed. And I told MBNA they could have 100 per cent of the PPI profits.

Matt and my Board all thought I was overdoing it – but Dave knew we were doing the right thing and we stuck to it, and have thanked our lucky stars ever since.

The new MBNA contract ensured we had enough cash flow to survive, so the third challenge was to find investors to support the rebuild of the Virgin One account.

Not long before, Paul Pester had opened Virgin Money in Australia. The business was a joint venture between Virgin Group and Macquarie. Westpac were providing a credit-card partnership.

Macquarie were not especially well known to the UK public, although they had launched an unsuccessful takeover bid for the London Stock Exchange in 2005 and they were a large and growing business, with a lot of ambition beyond Australia. Westpac were also not so well known outside Australasia, although they were the second biggest bank in both Australia and New Zealand.

The Virgin Group relationship with Macquarie was strong and there was a good relationship with the senior team in Sydney. So we asked Macquarie to support us in relaunching the Virgin One account in the UK.

Because Australians were already familiar with the current account mortgage product that the One account was based on, we had less explaining to do about just how good a product it could be for customers. Macquarie were ready to back both our new business and the Virgin brand – including our corporate ambition of making everyone better off.

So, my trips to Australia started again. Soon, we had broad agreement on a contract, a business, a product and a wholesale funding line.

It was exciting, and we built the Virgin Money team in anticipation of the relaunch.

I rang my Risk Director at RBS, Marian Watson, and asked her if she knew of anyone who would like to join Virgin Money as Risk Director. In her next breath, she made it clear that she herself would like to do that – and soon.

I called Norman McLuskie – who had always been so supportive of me as my boss at RBS – and asked if he would join our Board. He agreed straight away. Gordon McCallum was Chairman.

We had a strong team and we were ready to go.

One day in July 2007 we gathered the whole team together at the Kensington Roof Gardens in London. Richard Branson has owned this venue for many years and, to me, they epitomise his drive and spirit.

In the 1980s there was a nightclub (Regine's) in the building that now houses the Kensington Roof Gardens. One night in 1981 Richard queued up to get in and was turned away at the door for being too scruffy. He arranged a meeting with the club owner, and over a drink at the club Richard agreed, there and then, to buy the business. And he has owned it ever since – through thick and thin.

It felt like an auspicious place to talk with the team about our plans for the future, our deal with Macquarie and the way ahead. Not long after we had started the meeting I got an urgent call from one of the Macquarie team.

'The wholesale markets are shutting down,' he said. 'I'm afraid we are not going to be able to support you. We can't fund your plans for the new One account. We're pulling out of the deal.'

It was a momentous call.

Every single person in that room had given up safe jobs and risked their families' livelihoods to build this new Virgin business.

And now we had nothing.

The Run on the Rock

I am quite good at picking myself up from disappointments – but this was a big one.

Immediately we turned our attention to finding a new investor to see if this really was a market issue or an issue with Macquarie. It soon transpired that we were getting news about world markets and the impending financial crisis ahead of the game – this was just the tip of the iceberg.

A few weeks later, I went away for a night to Stobo Castle with my good friends Rosemary and Susan. We all had young daughters, and I remember a lot of our conversation was about the continuing story of Madeleine McCann's disappearance. We were all distressed about that, although pleased that Richard Branson had offered his help to clear the names of Madeleine's parents.

On the Sunday morning we were all wrapped in fluffy white dressing gowns, reading the papers.

The *Sunday Times* headlined the run on Northern Rock. It was a massive story on the front pages of all the papers – and inside continued with pictures of long queues of people outside Northern Rock branches, all wanting to take their money out. At this stage, it was hard to see beyond the run itself. There was speculation as to what had happened to cause Northern Rock to seek emergency funding from the government, but the real news was all about the impact on customers. I couldn't help but notice from the newspaper and subsequent TV coverage just how patient and present the Northern Rock staff were. Everyone who could help had pitched up to try to calm down the crisis.

An idea came to me there and then. Could we do something to help? I had run the RBS mortgage business, which was about the same size as Northern Rock, and, as a team, we had spent ages trying to analyse them as a competitor. And not only that, but who better to lead the recovery than Richard Branson?

I drove us all home that afternoon with those thoughts going around my head, and that evening I emailed a list of about twenty people, including Richard, suggesting that we should get involved.

Overnight, and into the next morning, nearly every one of the people on my email list tried to talk me out of it. Matt Baxby even walked over to see me very early in the morning to warn me that I was about to make a big fool of myself.

Only one person thought it was a good idea. Fortunately for me, that person was Richard Branson.

And as a result everyone lined up to help.

Richard called the Chancellor, Alistair Darling, that day, and got from him the telephone number I should call to discuss things further.

As I walked into my dining room that afternoon I saw a yellow Post-it note in the middle of the dark wooden table. The note had a number and a name on it.

And when I saw it I knew that I had got myself in the middle of something properly serious.

The number was that of the Governor of the Bank of England – Mervyn King.

Project Arrowa

We were going to call the Northern Rock adventure 'Project Arrow' – but someone made a typo and it became – and stayed – 'Project Arrowa'.

For me, Dave, Marian, Matt, Paul and Caroline, it was the banking journey of our lives.

We weren't the only ones looking at the business. A number of private equity firms saw the potential for a quick profit. As a result, most of the big investment banks were already tied up and we found ourselves supported by a smaller, boutique firm called Greenhill. The business was run by James – now Lord – Lupton and he assigned to us his lead banker, Edward Wakefield.

We were also well supported by the Virgin Group and a smaller advisory firm which was introduced by them – Quayle Munro, led by ex-Barings CEO, Peter Norris. Finally, Virgin Group introduced us to Andrew Ballheimer from Allen & Overy – one of the best lawyers at one of the best law firms in the business.

We realised that we had a lot to learn as we started to look at the Northern Rock business – and at its current issues.

It seemed to me and to the Virgin Money team, as we got deeper into the Northern Rock crisis, that everyone was speaking a different language. We discussed 'haircuts', 'mezzanine financing', 'trombone rights issues' and other exotic financial constructs. The kitchen-table test was needed more than ever.

The key issue was to work out how to fund the £100 billion Northern Rock business, now that retail deposits were being cashed in.

A huge proportion of the Northern Rock mortgage business had been securitised – meaning that mortgages were packaged up and sold as a block to external investors, so that the money lent to customers for their mortgages came from the wholesale financial markets.

The trouble was that, when those wholesale financial markets began to close as the global financial crisis started, Northern Rock could not be sure of being able to fund its loan book. And, once the media broke that story and fears mounted about Northern Rock's very survival, depositors started to remove their savings. So began the first run on a UK bank for generations.

There were two further complexities.

Firstly, the wholesale business was largely run through a huge 'Master Trust' called 'Granite'. 'Granite' had to be topped up with new mortgages as others were repaid – I have always thought of it as a monster that needed to be fed continuously – and this necessitated continued growth, which would be difficult in the face of the financial crisis and especially given the scale of the issues Northern Rock was facing.

Secondly, if the Northern Rock business could not maintain its credit rating at least at an A-level then, under its contracted terms, 'Granite' itself would collapse.

There was also a question over the credit quality of some of the mortgages that Northern Rock had written – especially the 'Together' product, which we had analysed before.

And we were still puzzled how a business that had such a significant share of the mortgage market could be doing so much better than competitors in terms of its arrears performance.

The task before us was Herculean. We were a tiny business with very few people trying to understand one of the biggest financial conundrums of the day and at the same time trying to save – and buy – Northern Rock.

But a fascinating thing happened as soon at the Virgin name became associated with the Northern Rock crisis. The outflow of retail deposits came to an abrupt halt. Customers, it seemed, believed that Virgin and Richard Branson could solve the problem, save the business and protect their money.

As a result of this customer behaviour, and the detailed work that we did to model the future of the business and to present our business plans, Virgin Money was made the preferred bidder in the race to save Northern Rock.

We knew that meant a huge amount of work ahead of us and James Lupton wanted to make sure that I got the best possible help and advice.

One Sunday afternoon James took me to meet Sir Brian Pitman at his home in St George's Hill, near Weybridge in Surrey. I had never been in a gated community before, and the houses and gardens were just fabulous.

Sir Brian – whom we always subsequently referred to as SBP – had been CEO and then Chairman of Lloyds Banking Group for many years and had experienced the secondary banking crisis of the 1970s. Back then, property price falls and interest rate increases meant that a number of smaller (secondary) banks were threatened with bankruptcy and had to be bailed out by the Bank of England. At one point, the crisis threatened to engulf even the National Westminster Bank. There was very little reference to the secondary banking crisis during all the coverage in 2007 and beyond, but there were important lessons to be learned.

Sir Brian had introduced the concept of 'shareholder value' to the City. He was a well-respected 'elder' and everyone – regulators, bankers and politicians – sought his views on how to handle the Northern Rock crisis.

That Sunday afternoon we sat in his living room drinking tea, while I presented Sir Brian with our business plans. He listened well and challenged hard.

'I'll think about it,' he said as I left, 'but I don't really think it's something I should get involved with. I think there's more coming than just this. They're in the depths of despair in New York.'

So I left feeling a bit deflated – but liking Sir Brian enormously.

The next day, James rang. 'Brian's said yes!' he said excitedly. 'You need to go and meet him in his London office.'

Sir Brian worked out of a townhouse near the US Embassy in London. Dave, Marian, Matt and I went to see him. We sat around a round table and he grilled us again on our plans.

'Okay,' he said, 'I'll help. I can see that you're serious and you know what you're doing. And I was thinking about Northern Rock. During the miners' strike they forgave many striking miners their mortgage payments. I think any bank that behaves like that deserves to be saved.'

And so we were off.

The wonderful thing for us was that we had full access to a bank that needed saving – without having been responsible for the problem. That meant that we could learn from the mistakes of others – and from the advice of many.

And more wonderful still, it seemed that everyone wanted to see Sir Brian – and he insisted on taking me to every meeting to which he went. As a result, I found myself, in quick succession, at the Bank of England, Her Majesty's Treasury, the House of Commons, the Financial Services Authority and numerous press offices.

I was always surprised at the number of people who joined these meetings – especially lawyers and bankers. Often there would be a 'second row' of chairs around the meeting table. What did all these people do? And why did so many need to turn up for a single meeting?

One Sunday afternoon we had a meeting in the offices of Slaughter & May, the lawyers who were representing the govern-ment. There were sixty-seven people in one room. I know because I counted them. Twice. Brian and I sat in the middle and there was standing room only at the back.

At one point, we broke up for private discussions and were ushered into a room with no chairs. I asked for one to be brought in. Brian was, after all, in his late seventies and we had been work-ing for hours already that day.

'Who's that chair for?' he asked.

'I thought you might like to sit down, Sir Brian,' I said.

'Is anyone else sitting down? Take it away!' he ordered.

On another occasion we went to meet George Osborne – then Shadow Chancellor – in Portcullis House. On his desk was a pack of 'Political Top Trumps' with all the current MPs and ministers in the pack. I was amused by it – and surprised when George Osborne asked if I would like to take the pack home. I refused, but was touched by the offer.

I was less amused one day when, flying from Edinburgh down to London, I saw Fred Goodwin two seats behind me on the BA flight to London City airport.

I agonised on the flight about whether I should talk to him and ask for his help with Northern Rock. After all, Emilio Botín, from Santander, had helped Fred with the NatWest deal. So I hung back and, as we crossed the tarmac at City airport, I asked Fred if he would help me with Northern Rock. 'No,' he said. 'It's a basket case.'

I asked if he would at least discuss my thinking with me, and he agreed to see me in his Gogarburn office in a few days' time. He was as good as his word.

I went to see Fred in his office in the Gogarburn Executive Suite soon afterwards. He looked unwell. His usual crisp, white shirt was crumpled and he was clearly under pressure. He was right in the middle of the ABN AMRO deal, in which the Dutch bank was acquired by a consortium that included RBS and Santander.

We had a cup of tea together, but we didn't get very far with any Northern Rock discussions.

As I left, I said to Fred, 'I must have got my timing very wrong. I joined you just after the NatWest deal, and left just before you complete on ABN AMRO.'

But, as time passed, I reflected that actually I might have got my timing very right indeed.

An EBO Business

In January 2008, with the Northern Rock crisis in full flow, Richard Branson was invited, along with a plane-full of other UK business-people, to accompany the then Prime Minister, Gordon Brown, on a trip to China.

Take-off was delayed as a result of a BA Boeing 777 crash-landing just over the perimeter fence at Heathrow, so both the plane and the airport were full of journalists.

At the same time, all parties who were interested in the Northern Rock deal were awaiting a term sheet to come through from the government's advisors, Goldman Sachs. A term sheet is an ini-tial document that outlines the terms and conditions of a business agreement. It was important to this deal as it would include details of the conditions of government and Bank of England support, which would be essential to help the new business to get off the ground.

I was at home in Edinburgh, watching the TV news, when a story came up about Richard Branson, the PM and the Northern Rock deal. The speculation was that Gordon Brown and Richard Branson were agreeing a 'sweetheart deal' for Northern Rock while on the plane from China.

Despite all of the headlines and the conspiracy theories, there wasn't any truth in the accusation and there was nothing at all 'sweetheart' about that period.

Indeed, the thing that I remember well is that, throughout more than six months of working almost twenty-four hours a day on the Northern Rock crisis and seeing regulators, civil servants and politicians on a regular basis, I never came across anyone – however powerful and mighty – who wanted to do anything other than their best to solve the problem, save the bank, support the Northern Rock staff and customers, and to help the country. I was surprised by that, but encouraged too. I came across professionalism, intellect and integrity, but those qualities rarely get an airing in the media.

As we worked hard to try and find a solution to the Northern Rock problem, I was spending time in London with Sir Brian. He always wanted to walk to every meeting if he possibly could, and I walked with him. It gave us time to talk and I loved hearing the stories of his life, his experiences and the people he had met.

He was a bit critical of the way the government were trying to solve this crisis. In his day, he said, bankers were called in to Downing Street, the doors were locked and no one was allowed out until the problem was solved.

He recalled one such meeting, convened by Norman Lamont, as Chancellor, one Christmas Eve. Brian remembered that the bankers all turned up 'in slacks and turtleneck jumpers' and couldn't wait to get home to their families for the festive season. That was the quickest solution to a banking crisis anywhere.

The crisis in Mexico took a few days longer to resolve.

One day, Brian received a call inviting him to Washington, with other world bankers, to try and find a solution to the Mexican financial crisis while Ronald Reagan was President.

All the bankers determined in advance that they were not going to use their balance sheets to bail out Mexico, and they agreed to stand strong together against such an outcome. After a day or two of meetings in Washington, the bankers left having achieved their objective and with their balance sheets intact.

They returned to their Washington hotels where, Brian recalled, on their beds was a note inviting them to the White House for drinks with the President in the Oval Office to thank them for their efforts and for their time. They went, and congratulated each other for not being pressurised into bailing out Mexico.

After drinks, President Reagan gave a thank-you speech. 'Gentlemen,' he said, for they were all male, 'thank you for coming to Washington and for your time here. I understand and respect your position. But you would be doing the United States of America a great favour if you would agree to support Mexico. All you need do is to sign in the book on the way out.'

Brian laughed as he said, 'Like lambs, as we left, every one of us signed, and Mexico was saved.'

In the end, despite all of the work from a set of fabulous teams, nothing was done to save Northern Rock.

It turned out, of course, that its ills were just the beginning of the great financial crisis that took hold across the globe in 2008. Northern Rock had been the first to suffer because it was so exposed to the wholesale financial markets.

I remember very clearly on a Sunday morning in February 2008, as I was watching Amy swimming, Ash rushed to the side of the pool and said: 'I've just seen the news. Alistair Darling has announced that they've nationalised Northern Rock.'

At that moment, it was a shock, for sure. We had worked night and day for months to put together a rescue package and there was no indication of nationalisation. And, despite all of our efforts, no one had warned Sir Brian or Sir Richard that this was going to happen. Gordon Brown called Richard straight after the announcement, but I understand that was to reduce the chances of Richard criticising the outcome, rather than to justify why Northern Rock should have been nationalised.

I suspect that it had been planned for quite some time and we were simply used as a helpful cover while the nationalisation scheme was put in place.

Whatever the truth, it was a terrible blow for Virgin Money.

Roland had done a great job at keeping the business operating well while the rest of us worked on Northern Rock. But we hadn't pursued any new developments or thought about any other strategy other than buying the bank.

And, to make matters much worse, the financial crisis now raging was likely to hinder any opportunities we may have had to bring in new investors.

While we had been working on Northern Rock, the US private equity firm, W.L. Ross & Co., run by Wilbur Ross, had been prepared to partner us in a successful deal, as had others. But the harsh truth was – no deal, no investors. They all went away.

And Virgin Group needed to protect itself, too. As a shareholder they were more likely to want money out of the business than to put it in. I had one piece of advice from Sir Brian ringing in my ears: 'Don't let Richard use you as a cash machine.'

In fact, we had already plugged a £40 million 'hole' in Virgin Money's finances and paid up a dividend of another £40 million, as a result of turning around Virgin Money's fortunes through our new credit-card deal.

And it was the credit-card business that we now looked to expand with MBNA in order to keep the business growing while we considered the future without Northern Rock.

The trouble was that we were employing too many people – especially in our IT team. We had increased some specialist areas very quickly, in order to build a new platform for mortgages and a new-style One account. If we had been brutal about it we should probably have made around fifty people redundant as we looked into the financial crisis – just to manage costs.

But, far from reducing costs, I was faced with a new commitment.

Only a week or two after Northern Rock was nationalised, Richard rang me. I was in our London offices – a tiny attic floor in a building off Dean Street in Soho.

'I've had a call from the London Marathon people,' he said. 'They'd like us to sponsor the marathon. Atlantic, Active and Media are already in and I hope you'll be able to be part of it too. It'll be fun and just right for the brand.'

To be honest, there was no chance we could afford to be a one-quarter sponsor when looked at rationally, but after the disappointment of Northern Rock it felt like just the boost we all needed to lift us up and give us a new direction.

From what I knew about the London Marathon, it was exactly the sort of organisation with which we wanted to be associated – it celebrated dedication, achievement, fun, community and charity support in a unique and inclusive way – and everyone I knew who had run the marathon eulogised about the whole experience.

Virgin Group were managing all the arrangements. We just had to find a quarter of the sponsorship money.

That is until, one by one, the other group companies dropped out, preferring, I think, to keep their cash as the credit crisis loomed.

I did not want another opportunity to go away so I said that we would sponsor the whole thing. Dave – and probably everyone else – thought I had gone mad. And it was certainly a pretty crazy thing to do in the circumstances.

We now had more than £3 million a year to find in addition to our normal expenses and on top of the staff costs we were carrying over and above current requirements.

It worried me. A lot.

We determined to find a way to make the commitment work and we turned to our EBO philosophy – to make 'Everyone Better Off' – to help us. How could we solve the many problems that faced us with something that worked for everyone?

As we looked deeper into the London Marathon, we focused on the way in which participants could raise money for charity. At the time, this was usually through the online sponsorship organisation, JustGiving. Runners could set up a page online and set out their chosen charity. JustGiving would collect the sponsorship from individual sponsors and transfer the cash to the charity of the runner's choice.

But here was the catch. JustGiving charged 5 per cent of all the money they collected as their fee. They also charged an additional 5 per cent on any tax relief that could be claimed on the donation. That meant that JustGiving could take up to 8 per cent, including the card-processing fee, of the total sponsorship money raised by London Marathon runners. It seemed scandalous then. And it still does today.

It was, if you like, our EBO moment.

As a financial services company, managing money is our core skill. So setting up a competing online donation business made complete sense. Building it would save every job at risk. And if we made it not for profit, then runners, sponsors and charities would be materially better off. And if we called it Virgin Money Giving then we would be developing our business at the same time.

By now, we'd established 'Everyone Better Off' as our main raison d'être. We had shortened it to EBO when we talked to each other. This was a step beyond the corporate social responsibility agenda that was part of big company culture – it was EBO in action.

The London Marathon team could see this too and swung into action to support us.

We put together a team of people and set about building a business, in a similar way to the style of the first Virgin Direct launch: plenty of late nights, simple and safe processes, and a focus on our three main customers – charities, fundraisers and sponsors.

We needed a Managing Director – someone with a flair for marketing and a desire to do the right thing – so I called Jo Barnett, who had been our Marketing Director at the Virgin One account. Jo and her husband, Jim, together with their three children, had moved to Canada just after RBS had bought the One account. I wasn't sure if she would be interested, but she flew back to the UK almost immediately to meet the team, and said yes straight away – I'm not sure at what point she mentioned her plans to Jim!

We sponsored our first London Marathon in 2010 and, by the time all the runners had crossed the line in 2016, Virgin Money Giving had processed more than £250 million (that's a quarter of a billion pounds!) of charitable donations – and all on a not-for-profit basis.

It brought the Virgin Money team together behind something we could all be proud of – and at a time when we needed it most.

Building Society

Our attempt to rescue Northern Rock had changed everything.

As a team, we had learned more about banking – good, bad, complicated, legal, financial, regulatory – than anyone could reasonably expect in the whole of their careers.

It no longer seemed that people were speaking a foreign language – but the kitchen-table test still applied. It seemed to me that some of the complexity masked important and simple realities. I have always tried to understand complicated banking issues in as simple a way as possible ever since.

Even more importantly, it was very clear that customers wanted to use Virgin in banking again. We had conducted a lot of research as we studied Northern Rock to see how consumers would respond to our brand in banking. It was a big deal, as the research findings were part of a business plan that was destined, or so we understood, for the Prime Minister's Red Box.

That research showed that more customers wanted to save with us than the Nationwide. More people wanted a mortgage with us than with Abbey National. And more consumers would have preferred to have had their current account with us than with NatWest.

It was a compelling strategic direction. People wanted us to offer a better bank. As a team, we knew now how to run one. And, given our focus on EBO, it also appealed to our sense of business purpose.

We went away together as a team, with my old MBA professor, Ronnie Lessem, and concluded that in missing out on Northern Rock we had lost a building society – but that we should now work out if we could somehow help with 'Society Building'. It sounded a little corny, and a bit worthy, but at the heart of our thinking was the need to remove some of the complexities that still surrounded financial services, and which had contributed so much to the banking crisis.

We needed a future that would allow a simple and straightforward business to make a difference to the world as well as making returns for shareholders.

And if that future was to be in banking then we needed to become a bank – and first we would need a banking licence.

That was much more difficult in 2009 than it is today. Not only did we need a clear plan, systems and a platform, but we also needed enough money – in the form of regulatory capital – to support our plans for the next five years. But with the financial crisis still raging that looked harder than ever.

A number of major tasks occupied us while the crisis was in full flow.

Firstly, the Virgin Group asked me, in addition to my UK role, to run the Virgin Money businesses in each of Australia, South Africa and the United States. Caroline took on these businesses as her full-time job and spent time living in both Australia and the US, and travelling in the meantime across four continents. I spent a lot of time in the air too.

The Australian business was exciting. We signed a new contract with Citigroup to support Virgin Money and enjoyed a very positive relationship with them.

On one occasion, we all decided to meet up in Hong Kong as the leaders of the Citi team were based there. It was arranged to coincide with the Hong Kong Rugby Sevens and we got tickets for the matches through our Australian offices.

After a meeting in a posh hotel with some senior, suave Citi people, most of the team headed off – rather awkwardly in an old bus with plastic seats – to the stadium. I followed behind the bus with the Head of Citi Australia – Roy Gori.

As we arrived, Caroline was racing out of the stadium in more distress and disarray than I have seen her before or since. It turned out that all the tickets sold through Australia were forgeries, and our important guests were being ejected by the Hong Kong police.

It all ended happily, but we did resolve never again to try and entertain important partners on their own turf.

Not long after, Matt Baxby, our Australian colleague who had dropped everything and arrived in Edinburgh in 2007, went back to Australia to run the Virgin Money business there. He did a great job, moved to Bank of Queensland – and in 2013 was part of the team that bought the Virgin Money business to be part of the Bank of Queensland group.

The US business was a different kettle of fish altogether.

There were two businesses in the United States; a peer-to-peer lending business, which had recently ceased taking on new business, and a mortgage pipeline business that took loans through to completion before selling them on, mainly to the enormous American mortgage banks Fannie Mae and Freddie Mac.

The business was based in Boston and was a partnership between Virgin and a private equity firm. It had more initial investment money than we had ever had in the UK – and much of it seemed to have been invested in large and well-appointed offices.

Caroline and others from the UK team spent months in Boston with a view to developing the business, based on all of our learnings from Northern Rock and RBS – but in the US context.

However hard they tried, the team found that the growth needed for Virgin Money to be profitable in the US outstripped the capital available during the financial crisis, and in the end we sold the business, in what was effectively a buy-out by local management.

In South Africa, Virgin Money was, and still is, a successful cards business with opportunities for growth – more recently it has started providing insurance products across South Africa.

The opportunities and issues in the overseas businesses kept us busy while the financial crisis raged.

But we needed even more focus back home.

The credit-card partnership with MBNA was continuing to thrive. In 2009 the partnership opened about 600,000 credit card accounts for new customers – taking one of the largest market shares of the year and maintaining very strong credit quality, despite the credit crunch.

As a result, MBNA wanted to discuss a new contract that would tie us to them for at least ten years. In return we would have a 50 per cent share of profits and losses on the Virgin Money-generated business.

It was a very valuable business deal for us and it was well received by the MBNA UK team who came to Edinburgh to sign the contract – another huge document and another big deal – over dinner in the Balmoral Hotel.

We were delighted. We had protected the financial interests of Virgin Money for many years to come. Or so we thought.

Our main aim continued to be building a UK bank. The question was whether to do that from scratch – or to see if we could acquire a small bank that already had a banking licence.

We planned for both options. After all, no one can be sure that any potential acquisition will actually happen, so it makes sense to plan for the alternative. Over the years, it has always been helpful to have a Plan B. And sometimes a Plan C and a Plan D.

We continually scoured the market for small banking operations and probably explored every single option available.

In the end, we landed on a tiny bank based in Yeovil, Somerset.

Church House Trust had been around for generations. It was established in 1792, and even boasted its own banknotes from all those years ago. It had only nine staff but they prided themselves on their customer relationships. They knew every mortgage – and pretty much every customer.

We decided to make an offer for Church House Trust, and to apply to the regulators for what is called a 'change of control', whereby all aspects of your plan, your business, your people, your systems and your finances are scrutinised before you can be approved to acquire a bank.

A senior member of the change-of-control team at the FSA called me one day as I was walking over the old green bridge into the back of Waverley station in Edinburgh.

'Are you sure you want to go down this route?' asked Graham. 'I know that we have to give you an answer within three months – but the answer could be no. Then you're back to square one. If you build from scratch, we can all take our time and you can be certain of getting approval – you just won't know when.'

I was very clear that we wanted to complete the acquisition. Having a three-month deadline for regulatory approval was important. We had seen so many *de novo*, or brand new, applications getting delayed for months – or even years.

We pushed on, and Sir Brian agreed to help us to put all of the necessary board and governance structures in place. Although, at that point, he would not agree to be my Chairman.

He had been approached by people he had known in the past to become Chairman on behalf of an investment company – known as NBNK – which was keen to look at buying bank assets in order to build a new UK bank. NBNK was especially interested in assets that the government was selling to satisfy State Aid rules – including Northern Rock.

Sir Brian met me in our London Jermyn Street offices. We had moved there after Sir Brian complained about having to step over the bodies of prostitutes to get into the door of our previous Soho offices. We walked together to see the NBNK team, who were based in a big London townhouse behind Savile Row.

As we walked there he said, 'I want you to think of being CEO if I become Chairman here. I know you're loyal to Richard but he won't pay you as well as they will. They will make you rich beyond your wildest dreams. You have to think of yourself.'

But I didn't really warm to the team, and I could not see any equivalent to EBO in their approach. And, whatever my loyalty to Richard, I was also 100 per cent loyal to the Virgin Money team and to the business we were building, so moving on was not an option. And it is never a good thing to make a decision just because of money.

I told Brian that afternoon, and I don't think he was surprised. Ash thought I should have given it more thought – but he too knew that Virgin Money was already far more than just a job for me, and for the vast majority of people with whom I was lucky enough to work.

The question then became how to raise the money we needed to buy Church House Trust, and to capitalise it to meet regulatory requirements. In total, we needed £50 million. And, remember, this was to sct up a bank in the middle of the banking crisis.

I spent a lot of time meeting private equity firms in London and in New York, and there was a lot of interest.

But we never forgot how important it is to have a Plan B, and so I started to talk to MBNA about them advancing us £50 million from the new contract – in effect providing money now prior to it being earned in the future.

I will always be grateful to the MBNA team who made that happen. Because, at almost the last moment, our potential private equity backers pulled out and we were, once again, looking defeat in the face.

So we asked MBNA to advance the £50 million we needed before we had our final meeting with the FSA to seek their approval to our change-of-control application on 9 October 2009.

We had done everything we could to be ready for the meeting. We always plan, replan, think again, simplify the issue, and try to see angles we haven't seen before.

But we could do no more to get the money. That was squarely in MBNA's hands. And it was becoming clear that it was by no means a done deal.

We were all in London, in the Jermyn Street offices, on 8 October to prepare for the meeting next day. By 11 p.m. we hadn't yet heard from MBNA, and Roland sent me to the hotel we were booked into in Canary Wharf, so as to be close to the FSA for the 9 a.m. meeting next morning.

When I arrived, he had even had a glass of white wine sent to the room. The hotel had big windows looking over the river and the curtains were open and the bright city lights of London looked like fairy lights in the distance.

I went to bed, sipped the wine and looked out at the lights – wondering if our plans for tomorrow would amount to anything and rehearsing the messages I would have to deliver if they didn't. But about 3 a.m. I got a phone call from Pete Ball at MBNA.

'It's done,' he said. 'We've released the money.'

Next morning, Marian and I set off for the FSA with our new Finance Director, Finlay Williamson. Finlay had worked with us all at RBS and Dave felt that it was important that someone who had been a Finance Director in a big bank took on the role once we had a banking licence – not least because the next steps were critical and Dave was needed as our Strategy Director to make sure we navigated them well.

I am surprised that I can't remember that seminal meeting with the FSA. It must be because, after that stressful night waiting for MBNA to release the money, I knew that our change of control would be approved.

And it was.

By the end of that week we had acquired Church House Trust and had a full banking licence.

Raising that first £50 million had been one of the hardest hurdles so far. Later, I was able to see that it was far harder than raising the next billion.

Not long after, I was sat at home reading a book one evening when my mobile phone rang.

A gruff American voice said, 'Jayne-Anne? Wilbur Ross here. Well done buying that bank. We've been watching you and we're keen to support you. Let's get together and you can tell me your plans.'

The fact is that you never know who is watching and where the next opportunity will come from. Wilbur Ross is one of America's most successful investors, has run a number of big businesses in the States, and is, at the time of writing, awaiting formal appointment as the US Commerce Secretary. He is definitely what you would call a serious player.

Within the next few months Wilbur Ross had invested over £100 million and acquired just over 20 per cent of the Virgin Money business. And, more importantly, we now had the financial capability to do the things we wanted to do.

The question was – what to do next? We knew we had the capability to do great things. We had strong backing and a team who were ambitious to deliver something that was truly EBO.

With a new future ahead of us we needed bigger offices in Edinburgh. We had moved out of my dining room a couple of years earlier and into one floor of a small office building with glamorous views of Edinburgh Waverley railway station. But we needed somewhere bigger and somewhere that would allow us to grow.

We soon found the right place: a beautiful, Georgian, redbrick building on the corner of St Andrew Square, right in the heart of Edinburgh. Not only was the building great, but the irony of being on the same square that accommodated the original RBS head office I had visited so often as we planned the launch of the Virgin One account was not lost on us.

The only problem was the Edinburgh planning laws, which protect the historic façades of buildings in Edinburgh's New Town. They required us to keep the individual oak-panelled rooms on the first floor of the building if we were to take owner-ship of the newly modernised open-plan offices above. We could not imagine how we would use such rooms and keep our open culture intact.

One afternoon, a few of us stood in the panelled rooms and remembered that, when we were at RBS, they had closed a women-only branch on Princes Street. The ladies of Edinburgh had revolted because they used to meet there for a cup of tea after a hard day's shopping.

The thought inspired us to think of making the panelled rooms available to our Edinburgh customers.

The concept of the Virgin Money Lounge was born. It was an idea inspired by EBO and, we felt, could not be copied, credibly, by any other bank. Our lounge idea was, we felt, legitimised by the airline lounges that Virgin Atlantic so successfully hosted.

I was nervous proposing such an idea to my Board. We had no business plan for the lounge and it was certainly a novel idea. I had no need to worry. Both Gordon McCallum and Patrick McCall, the Virgin directors, thought it was a great idea and persuaded the rest of the Board to take the risk.

We asked Caroline to take responsibility for making the set-up suitable for our customers, and soon we had a magnificent space with three beautiful rooms with TV, dining room, posh toilets and a grand piano exclusively for the use of Virgin Money customers. We agreed the lounge should not be a commercial venture. It was to be a retreat for our customers and their guests.

But very soon, partly as a result, sales in the Edinburgh store a few streets away went through the roof. By the end of that year sales were up 300 per cent. We have continued to open lounges ever since and now have seven around the UK. In 2016 those lounges welcomed over half a million customers.

Meanwhile, now that we had bought Church House Trust, it was more important than ever to find a Chairman who was an experienced banker. Sir Brian Pitman had continued to give me all the support I needed and I met him often to absorb all the wisdom he could share with me. I had not given up hope of him becoming Virgin Money's Chairman, despite NBNK continuing to court him.

Finally he agreed.

The whole Board was delighted. We had a dinner at the Haymarket Hotel in London with Sir Brian to celebrate. The news leaked – I know not how – and it was the headline in the *Financial Times* next morning.

We got down to business straight away.

Brian was very clear that the biggest risk we ran as a privately owned bank was of the two shareholders – Virgin and Wilbur Ross – wanting to drive profit at the expense of risk management.

I knew Virgin Group would not do that. Despite being an entrepreneurial businessman, Richard had always done things right. And the Virgin brand simply could not tolerate a failed bank as part of the group – so they wanted to manage risk cautiously.

But a US private equity firm was a different question. We simply did not know how they would behave.

Brian was insistent. 'We will have the shareholders at the Group Board, but not on the Bank Board, and certainly not at the Committees. That way they can influence the direction of the business and protect their investment – but the independent directors must run the bank and make sure it is properly governed.'

The Committees are an important part of the governance of any well-run bank. They look after key decisions on remuneration, risk, auditing, pricing and so on, so it is essential that they sit separately to the Board and operate as independently as possible to avoid conflicts of interest. So Sir Brian's guidance made complete sense to me, and both shareholders agreed to the approach at the Board meeting in February 2010.

Brian never had to raise his voice to make a point. His years of experience and success just meant that the Board and both share-holders held him in the utmost respect, and agreed with his way of doing things.

He was pleased with the way the Board went, and I asked him why he had decided to become our Chairman.

'Because,' he said, 'in all the work I did about driving shareholder value it was obvious that the businesses that treat their customers well are the ones that do best. You've taken that further with your EBO approach and you'll do well.'

We agreed to meet a few days later. Just before then, Amy was appearing in a show in Edinburgh, and he rang to wish her well.

I never heard from him again.

That night, at a Board dinner, Sir Brian collapsed, and he died a few days later.

His funeral was attended by many of the big names in banking, and St Paul's Cathedral was packed for his memorial service. George Osborne, then Chancellor of the Exchequer, represented the govern-ment. It was striking to see that so many people came to pay their respects to a truly great man.

I had learned lots from him – but I wished that we'd had time to talk more.

His obituaries described him as the most successful, important, outstanding and respected banker of his generation. He is missed by many, and very much by me.

Chapter 6

NORTHERN ROCK ... AND BEYOND!

2010–2016

'This is our offer to acquire Northern Rock,' I said.
'It would be rude not to take it now that you've written
it', he replied.

Who Cares Wins

I T BECAME obvious that there were three different acquisition opportunities available to us to expand the Virgin Money business after the financial crisis, all of which involved us acquiring a bigger bank and growing it on the foundations of the Church House Trust banking licence.

The privatised Northern Rock would need to be sold at some point. Meanwhile, to meet State Aid rules, RBS was required to sell 318 branches in England and Wales (that part of the business became known as Williams & Glyn), while Lloyds Bank needed to offload TSB.

We looked at all three of the options in great detail. Towards the end of summer 2010, I took the Virgin Money management team up to Gleneagles to consider which option we should commit to. In the end we decided that RBS had too many technology issues, and that Lloyds was selling too many branches. In contrast, we had followed Northern Rock over the years since nationalisation and it fitted our plans perfectly.

The trouble was, it wasn't for sale. Yet.

In October 2010, Dave, Gordon McCallum and I went to see UK Financial Investments (UKFI) – the government entity in charge of selling Northern Rock. At that time, UKFI had offices just off Trafalgar Square.

We were shown into a big office with a huge table and far too many chairs. Robin Budenberg, who ran UKFI at the time, arrived, and I placed on the table in front of him a letter in a sealed envelope.

'This is our offer to acquire Northern Rock,' I said.

Robin looked shell-shocked, and we talked about our thought process and our proposal. After almost an hour, he was still eying the unread letter on the table.

'It would be rude not to take it now that you've written it,' he said.

We left it with him. And waited, for the next several months, for something to happen.

Robin subsequently told me that 'the letter changed everything'. Of course, putting in a letter to purchase Northern Rock outside any official sales announcement was an audacious move. But, as a result, UKFI and Northern Rock got themselves ready for a sales process.

Life had not been easy for people working within Northern Rock – there had been a succession of contract managers and con- sultants in and out of the Gosforth head office for several years, and staff felt as if they had been treading water, without any clear direction on where to go next.

By early summer 2011 the 'bad bank' of Northern Rock had been separated from the 'good bank' in accordance with State Aid rules, and an Information Memorandum, containing the data any purchaser would require to analyse the business, was made available to potential buyers – including Virgin Money.

On 15 June, George Osborne formally announced that Northern Rock was ready to be sold.

We made it the number one business priority and threw ourselves into the process. Greenhill were once again our banking advisers. Allen & Overy were once again our lawyers, led by Andrew Ballheimer. The team dusted off our knowledge from the past and we were ready to go. Best foot forward.

At that precise time, Ash and I were having our house renovated and had rented a small but glitzy flat in Edinburgh. I was in the bedroom of the flat when a call came through from Keith Morgan of UKFI to say that our offer was not good enough, but that he would like to meet up. I went down to London and immediately realised that I could work with Keith.

Over the coming weeks we improved our offer and agreed a deal.

Those few words belie the enormous effort it took to align Virgin, Wilbur Ross, UKFI and the Virgin Money management team.

It was an enormous undertaking, but we got there.

And I think that was for one reason only. Keith and I agreed that this was so complicated and so sensitive we could do it only with sensible collaboration. That did not mean that either side caved in to the other. But it did mean that we worked together to resolve the many complex issues in a collaborative way.

Freshfields were the government's lawyers. They were represented by a long-in-the-tooth and combative lawyer, Barry O'Brien. Barry was good and ready to negotiate hard.

In my own team, Stephen Pearson had joined previously from RBS as our General Counsel. I had bumped into him at City Airport one day on the way up to Edinburgh and we had swapped stories. I asked him to pop in to Virgin Money for a coffee and, when he did a few days later, I offered him a job. He left saying he would think about it.

He subsequently told me that he had never intended to join us, but when he got back to his RBS desk it felt like a prison. I think it helped our cause that Stephen had been spending his time sorting out the legalities of the growing list of shareholder lawsuits against RBS (which are still going on more than six years later). He told me that he would rather help to build a new bank than carry on defending a broken one.

Stephen rang me and agreed to join.

Working with Stephen has always been a joy. He is collaborative, fair and balanced, and guided by integrity and his own moral code, which is completely consistent with EBO.

That was important that Sunday in Freshfields with Barry and with Andrew Ballheimer. The lawyers started to get into a particular point and it was getting heated.

I said to Keith: 'I thought we agreed this would be collaborative?'

The tone changed. We agreed a way forward that worked positively for all parties. We took a similar approach with the banks – Greenhill on the Virgin Money side, and Deutsche Bank with UKFI – establishing an agreement to work for a positive outcome for both parties, and to trust each other.

I could tell from the initial reactions that this was an unusual way of working – but it was successful. Everyone worked hard to resolve every point.

Astonishingly, the news did not reach the media, despite hundreds of people – including regulators, bankers, lawyers and politicians in the City and beyond – knowing what was going on.

Mark Hoban, the City Minister, called me in to the Treasury to see him.

He had a large corner office overlooking Horse Guards Parade with big squashy sofas in it – but I sat directly opposite him across his huge oak desk.

'We've come a long way with the contract,' he said. 'But there are a few things you and I need to agree together.'

I was worried that this could be the end of the deal, but Mark said: 'First, I want you to agree to no redundancies for at least three years after you've bought Northern Rock – and no branch closures either. I want you to look me in the eyes and tell me now that you will pay me the interest due on any money the government leaves in. And I want you to do all you can to support the Northern Rock Foundation.'

All of these points seemed absolutely right to me and I readily agreed – there and then, without recourse to my Board. It seemed to me that all of the Minister's requests were, in a nutshell, EBO.

By this time, Sir David Clementi had agreed to become the Virgin Money Chairman. Sir David had enjoyed an extensive career in finance, first working at Kleinwort Benson before being appointed Deputy Governor of the Bank of England, then moving on to be Chairman of the Prudential.

He had considered joining us earlier, soon after Brian Pitman had died, but decided against it, having been made Master of the Mercers – the second largest City of London Guild which, to my surprise, had been created by the largesse of the real Dick Whittington in the fourteenth century, and which is still going strong today as a philanthropic body.

After his year in office was over, I revisited Sir David in his offices in St James's and found him shouting at the television, as politicians made their arguments before the general election of 2010.

I liked the passion he showed, and I think he liked the fact that I had waited over a year for him to be Virgin Money's Chairman. He agreed to join just before we made our offer for Northern Rock.

On the day we made the offer, Edward Wakefield was five minutes late in producing the Offer Letter for Sir David to sign and was subject to similarly loud treatment as that reserved for the politicians on TV. A proper dressing down indeed.

And I was subject to similar challenges from Wilbur Ross as we finalised the deal. He was right on top of every detail and kept me on my toes.

There were lots of phone calls where Wilbur clearly and bluntly expressed his views. There were often many very quiet people also on the call, who listened while I explained my position and justified – as far as I could – the deal construct. It can be lonely as a CEO.

It was a loud, stressful and vibrant time.

But finally we made our offer, which, in the end, totalled £1 billion for the acquisition of the 'good bank' of Northern Rock.

On the night of 16 November 2011 I was at Freshfields' offices ready to sign the deal. The contract was delivered from Downing Street, personally signed by the Chancellor, George Osborne.

But our banks had hit a stumbling block. One of the syndicate was unable to get all of the Credit Committee approvals it required.

Stephen and I tried to stay calm.

A vast number of calls were made. Doors were slammed. Meetings were held.

Well past the eleventh hour, the required agreement came.

We had the money. I could sign the contract next to the Chancellor's signature.

It was an amazing moment.

Next morning, the whole Virgin Money deal team assembled in our Jermyn Street boardroom. Sky News was on. They had heard that the Chancellor was going to make an important announcement but, because it had been kept so tight, they did not know what it was about. The cameras were trained on the doors of Number 11 Downing Street.

The Chancellor emerged. 'I am pleased to announce,' he said, 'that yesterday we reached an agreement to sell Northern Rock to Virgin Money.'

It was a long journey getting to this point. And I knew then that this was just the beginning.

Project Sapphire

After pulling off the deal of our lives, we now had a balance sheet of almost £20 billion and 3,000 people to look after.

As Roland had once said to me – years earlier and when we were much smaller – 'look how many people's lives we affect'. The thought has always stayed with me. Running a business brings responsibilities way beyond the bottom line.

We also had three million customers to care for. We had written to them to see how they felt about Virgin Money buying Northern Rock. About 100,000 people replied and all were positive. Interestingly, the vast majority of customers who wrote in urged us, first and foremost, to look after the people.

On the day that the deal was announced, customers rang to congratulate staff because, after all the problems of the past, they had a future again. And people wrote in to us to urge us to look after the branch staff who had looked after them and their money for years.

It reminded me of Sir Brian Pitman's words all those years ago. He remembered that Northern Rock had supported the striking miners by deferring their mortgage payments and said that 'a bank that behaves that honourably deserves to be saved'.

Our experience has always been that if you try to do the right thing, and if you look after your people, everything else follows. EBO in action.

And, of course, that brings with it a commitment from everyone to get together, to work hard and to make the business a success.

But a bank is a complex organisation, and one with the history of Northern Rock needed to be well understood to be well managed and well led. During the acquisition process, our team had spent hundreds of hours studying details and data, and had been given full access to interview the Northern Rock management team.

However, we were still a long way off what you would call a full understanding of how the business worked.

I was especially worried about how we would be received by the north-east in general and by the staff in particular. Northern Rock had been a major part of the regional economy for years. It had provided housing for families and thousands of jobs for workers. The local community had been proud of its success and were devastated by its demise.

So, we took over the business with some trepidation and tried to be as respectful as we could be of the brand, the people and the processes that we had acquired.

In May 2012 we held our first staff opinion survey to see how we were doing. The resounding feedback was 'make us more Virgin'! And so, with the permission and encouragement of the staff, we were properly off.

I had underestimated the fact that the Northern Rock team had worried about their future for the best part of five years. Many had spent their working lives trying to do the right thing for their customers but, since the crisis, had done so without a clear objective or strategy.

Now the opportunity for a new start with a new brand was real and exciting.

It was important that we got it right. So we tried to make sure that we left nothing to chance as we delved into the complexities of the systems, processes, capital, liquidity, products, pricing, costs and arrears.

Time and again we asked the stupid question. I certainly did.

To start with, people thought that was because I was indeed stupid. Maybe I am. But soon we found lots of things that could be improved, made more efficient or just done away with.

It was hard work but slowly we started to get to grips with all the complexities of the business and to make sure we were in control.

We were making good progress when, one Sunday afternoon in the summer of 2012, still in Our Hat in Edinburgh, I took a phone call from Ian O'Doherty and Michele Greene at MBNA.

'We wanted to warn you,' they said, 'that Bank of America are going to announce tomorrow that they are selling the MBNA UK business. The CEO wants to concentrate on the US cards business and sell everything else off.'

It was a massive blow.

Having bought the loss-making Northern Rock, our Virgin Money credit-card business was keeping everything afloat financially while we turned the bank around. And we had enough on our plates to manage our new acquisition without being thrown immediately into another deal process.

I felt let down, angry and, frankly, very scared. But there was nothing for it but to get on with it.

Part of the problem was the ten-year contract that we had signed with MBNA a few years ago and which had helped us to buy Church House Trust.

The terms were favourable to Virgin Money and so MBNA needed to get us out of that contract fast so that they could sell the rest of the business to another buyer.

As a result, the looming threat was that they would, within the contract, support us less and less, and force us to sell uncompetitive products, unless we released them from their contractual obligations.

We had spent every available penny on acquiring Northern Rock and, having just bought a bank with £14 billion of secured mortgages, adding our credit-card portfolio of £3 billion of unsecured lending was just too risky.

So we made an offer to acquire £1 billion of the Virgin Money card book on terms which we could afford, and which released MBNA from our contract, so that they were free to rebrand and then to sell the rest of the portfolio – and their entire business.

The trouble was that, having bought £1 billion of cards, we did not have a card business to which to migrate them. We would have to build one ourselves. From scratch. And then we would have to undertake a complex migration from MBNA systems to our own.

No organisation had ever done that before. Plenty had set up credit-card businesses. Even more had migrated cards portfolios to their existing systems. But we never found any other company that had done both at the same time.

But, in spring 2013, we completed on the deal. We had no choice if we wanted to protect our business and to keep as many customers as we could.

We agreed that MBNA would administer our business for us until we could operate our own. The trouble was that they charged a mark-up that grew over time – a penalty, if you like, that got more expensive the longer it took us to set up our own operations.

The strain on everyone in early 2013 was immense. And to top it off, our Board felt we should be building a new current account product.

As a small team, managing our money carefully, we were faced with running an efficient bank, building a credit-card business from scratch, and now getting a project off the ground to build a complicated product – a full current account.

I should, of course, have said that we couldn't do it all. But the Board were unforgiving. As one director said to me, 'If you can't find a way to build a current account, then I will find a CEO who will.' Tough times indeed.

And those times got tougher when Project Sapphire, which we had set up to build the cards business, ran into trouble.

We had underestimated the cost and skills needed to build our own cards business and, in summer 2013, it became clear to me that we had a problem. And we needed a whole team of credit-card experts to solve it.

And that is when I called Michele Greene at MBNA to see if she would join us to build our credit-card business. To be honest, I was not optimistic that she would leave MBNA and come to us.

She came to see me in my newly renovated Edinburgh house one night and, over a glass of wine, we talked about what needed to be done. Not long after, she came to look around our Gosforth offices and could see the potential for the business.

And, in much the same way as I had left RBS with a team of people who wanted to rebuild the Virgin One account, Michele and a brilliant team of cards experts – who bought into EBO and who wanted to change the world – exchanged life at a big bank for life at Virgin Money.

I don't know what we would have done without Michele and her fabulous team.

They took on the most complex project we had ever attempted and worked round the clock for many, many months to get it done. I would like to say that it was straightforward and fun. It was neither.

It was massively complex, all-consuming work that required a super-human effort from everyone involved. It drove lots of the team to despair along the way.

But we did it. And we learned that there are two special qualities that you need to build a bank – an entrepreneurial attitude, which implies devoting yourself, beyond reason, to the task in hand, whatever it takes – and to be an expert in your subject.

In banking I have realised that it is very, very hard to find both of these qualities in people.

People who have worked in big banks tend to be narrow specialists. And they tend not to have had to make the personal sacrifices that need to be made to get a new and complex business off the ground.

But the MBNA cards team had built their own business in exactly that way over the years – and had put in countless hours of effort to make that business a success.

And now they were at Virgin Money. We were very, very lucky indeed.

Creating a Crisis

The first few months of 2014 were undoubtedly the hardest of my professional life so far.

Lee Rochford had joined us in October 2013. Lee had been an investment banker and had supported us well over the years from his role at RBS, when we needed to raise debt. We asked him to join as CFO to bring his experience of bank balance sheets and of the stock markets, as we prepared ourselves for listing.

But, as he said himself, he was not a qualified accountant.

Producing the year-end accounts for 2013 was therefore a difficult process, especially as we aimed to produce full listed company disclosure for the first time in preparation for when we made our entrance on the markets.

The business was doing well but we were still getting over the original false start in the cards business. It proved to be a minor glitch as, in the end, Michele and her team delivered a brilliant result, on time, on budget and on plan in 2015. But initially the Board had been unforgiving. 'You've crashed the fucking car!' said one of my directors, unhelpfully. I knew we hadn't. But our Board were used to us being only successful on all fronts from day one.

And we still had not got an all-singing, all-dancing current account out there. The reason was that it is impossible, as all our competitors have found, to launch a new current account, at scale, into a market that offers 'free banking' and still make sufficient profit to protect capital, let alone to make a reasonable return.

So we started to look at how we could have a current account to be proud of and still make it a top performer – even with limited volumes.

We decided to launch our 'Essential Current Account' – the best basic bank account in the market.

A basic bank account is defined by regulation. It has to be fee-free, with no hidden catches, and an overdraft facility is not allowed. The aim is to bring people into the banking system who so far have not had a bank account. The accounts are loss making, so they are not particularly well supported by the big banks.

Once again, ours was an EBO solution. We could offer á great account and manage volume by offering it only through our seventy-five branches. That would bring a top-notch product to customers who needed it, give us experience of operating a current account on a safe and gradual basis and – we thought – satisfy the Board's desire for Virgin Money to offer what Americans call a 'checking account'.

As I write, this account has been recognised as one of the best basic bank accounts in the UK.

Our credit-card business is thriving as a growing operation following the extraordinary, complex and hugely successful migration of the credit cards we had bought from MBNA.

And our Financial Statements are documents that I am still boring enough to be proud of – for their full disclosure, their presentation, and for the results they support.

But, back in early 2014, progress on these issues was not fast enough for some directors. And, because we were still a private company, there was real tension between what some of the shareholders wanted and the independent governance of a bank.

I thought back to Sir Brian Pitman's advice: 'Keep the shareholders on the Group Board focused on strategy. The independent directors need to run the Bank Board and the Committees.'

It was a hugely stressful time for me. The challenge was to satisfy the Board's desire to build a full range of banking products within our financial and operational capabilities while running what was, let's face it, the old Northern Rock safely and acquiring a new credit-card business all at the same time. It was a tough ask and a big risk.

I called a friend of mine, Andy, who had run a business psychology firm for years and talked him through my dilemma. Should I resign from the business I had built and loved for twenty years? Was I being unreasonable to try and slow things down? How could I realign the business and the Board so that we didn't break anything – or anybody?

Pushing ahead on all fronts felt like a big risk, and the lessons we had learned from the financial crisis made me feel that I had to stand my ground. I had no intention of presiding over another problem bank – and especially not one based on the lessons and history of Northern Rock.

When I spoke to Andy, he told me that he had helped several CEOs to deal with similar issues over the years.

'The way forward,' he said, 'is to create a crisis. That way the issue has to get resolved one way or another. What I can't tell you is which way it will go. You've got to be prepared for a tough time and for the outcome to go against you.'

We sat down as an executive team and decided this was the only way forward. So we stuck to our plans and continued to build and deliver the bank in a controlled and sensible way.

If I got it wrong, my job was on the line, for sure.

Then, late one Sunday evening, I got an email from Richard Branson. 'I want you to come to Necker tomorrow' was all that it said.

Ash and I were watching television, and as I read it out to him we both knew that this was where 'creating the crisis' had taken me. This was the route to resolution – one way or the other.

All of my career, Ash has always hated the last-minute changes in my diary, in my travel and in my life that go with running a business like Virgin Money. He is usually cross about it.

But this time was different.

'We'd better get you packed then,' he said.

You May Know Me as Richard. But Now I'm Going to be Frank

While we were packing that Sunday night for the trip to Necker Island next morning, I rang Caroline.

'This is it,' I said. 'We'll get everything sorted out now, one way or another.'

Caroline booked the flights for me. It was a difficult task as the schedule was tight and I was 'live' on *BBC Breakfast* first thing. It was an interview in Edinburgh with Steph McGovern. We were on a balcony looking out over the castle and the funny thing was that she and I were wearing identical jackets – black with white piping. That got picked up in the papers next day, more so than the topic of our discussion.

But by then I had arrived on Necker Island. It had been an extraordinary journey – by any standard.

I got the British Airways flight from Edinburgh down to Gatwick so that I could connect straight through to the Barbados flight.

As the plane waited on the tarmac in Edinburgh, I rang Gordon McCallum.

'What's all this about?' I asked.

'It's important,' he said. 'We are at a crisis point. It's your opportunity to talk it through with Richard. Good luck.'

The Edinburgh flight was late into Gatwick. The gate we arrived at turned out to be literally next to the one I needed for Barbados. But to get to it I had to get a bus from the Edinburgh plane and go through domestic arrivals. Then I had to re-enter the airport and go through passport control and then security again.

Then I had to run – literally – through the airport to get back to where I had first started – and the Barbados flight.

The flight was closing – flashing red – but, because we had booked straight through from Edinburgh, my PA, Emma, was on the phone to BA, begging them to wait since it was the late arrival of my connecting flight that had caused the problem.

When I arrived at the gate – red as a beetroot, flustered and untidy – they were waiting for me. It was thirteen minutes after departure time. I boarded the plane, sat down and we started to taxi to the runway.

Thank you, BA! The irony of me thinking that on a trip to see Richard Branson was not lost on me.

As we flew out over the Atlantic, all sorts of thoughts were going through my head – but I felt remarkably calm, sure as I was that all the decisions that we had been making had been the right ones for the business, for our customers and for the Virgin brand.

When I landed in Barbados there was a tiny plane waiting for me. It had four seats and a basket of fruit in the back. It was not much bigger than my car at home.

We flew over green islands and the bright blue Caribbean Sea and, about two hours later, landed at Tortola in the British Virgin Islands.

I came out of the airport and saw Eustace, a member of the Necker Island staff, waiting for me.

We walked down to the harbour and jumped (well, Eustace jumped – I was less athletic) into a white speedboat with white leather seats and a full cool box.

I had a Diet Coke, because I had forgotten that it is almost impossible for the unpractised to drink anything on a speedboat. True to inelegant form, the drink was all over me by the time we arrived.

We sped through the beautiful seas and I admired anew the islands along the route. We passed Moskito Island and I could see the ongoing building where Richard was creating his new house.

Then, as night fell, we were there.

We arrived at the red dock and I was greeted by a lovely woman called Kat.

'Hi, Jayne-Anne,' she said. 'I'm sorry I'm dressed like this. We've got guests in the great house and they're having a Greek night.'

I didn't tell her that, given my somewhat extraordinary day, I had not even noticed that she was dressed in a toga with a golden laurel headpiece.

Kat drove me up to Richard's private house on the island. He was there on his own and showed me to my room. It is a beautiful room with a huge white bed on a raised platform, looking out through massive windows across the island to the beautiful blue sea.

The whole room is made out of wood and decorated a calm white. The huge chairs are soft, white and welcoming. The mosquito net makes the crisp, white, linen-dressed bed feel like a safe cocoon.

Behind the bed is a door to the outside bathroom with an enormous stone bath – with a rubber duck sat on the side – and a shower encased in island stone with just the wild greenery of the island to protect your modesty.

As I unpacked and changed, I thought, not for the first time, what a privilege it was to be in this place – whatever the circumstances.

I went out to join Richard for a drink before dinner. He was sat in his favourite chair next to the pool with the round great room behind him. Richard suggested that we share a bottle of his favourite rosé wine, called Whispering Angel.

'Okay,' he said. 'We've worked together for twenty years and you've never let me down. What on earth's going on?'

And I told him the whole story. How we had all worked so hard to get to an EBO place. How we were dealing with the pressures created out of Board demands. How our achievements were not being recognised. How we were trying to steer between drastically conflicting elements of risk and reward.

I realised, as we spoke, that we don't often listen well. Certainly, I don't listen that well, but Richard actively listened to me – and took notes – in a way that I have never experienced before. He didn't offer any comments. He just listened.

After an hour or so we moved over to the other side of the deck for dinner. It was a Greek meal – on the menu for the party up at the main house.

We carried on talking over dinner and beyond.

Finally, Richard got up. 'I'm off to bed now,' he said. 'Come and watch me play tennis in the morning.'

I went to bed and rang Dave, who was anxious to know what was going on. I really wasn't sure what sort of an update I could give him.

Despite my long day and night I was up early next morning and walked down to the tennis courts with Richard – past Bali Lo, a beautiful house where Ash and I had stayed twice before, past two truly enormous tortoises, through the sandy track to the tennis courts, close to the beach.

The tennis coach was there and I watched Richard playing for a while before, at Richard's suggestion, heading off for a walk along the beach and up over the rocky, undeveloped side of the island.

The beauty of the place is breathtaking, and every time I am there I marvel at the extraordinary vision of one man and how he could have created something so unique in just a few decades.

We met back at the house for breakfast in the shade.

'What would you like for breakfast?' asked Richard.

I have learned that, when you are out of your depth, the best thing is to copy your host. 'Whatever you're having,' I said.

And we had hard-boiled eggs, toast and jam, and a big cup of tea.

'Okay,' said Richard. 'I've thought about everything you've said. I'm a hundred per cent behind you as CEO. Go home, and while you're flying, think about what you want to do next and give me a call.'

So, less than twenty-four hours after I had arrived, I made the return journey back to Edinburgh, my mind whirring. What was the right thing to do next?

And then, on the long flight back from Barbados, it came to me.

When we had bought Northern Rock on 1 January 2012 we had all agreed that we would list the business, or float it on the stock market, in 2015, after we had published three years of financial accounts. That meant starting the process around April 2015, which was almost a year away.

But, in my heart of hearts, I knew that the business was in great shape and ready for listing now.

As I thought about it, I realised that a commitment to list earlier than planned would solve everything. The pressures we had experienced had all really been about getting the business stable and ready for listing. Getting the listing done now would bring the Board together around a common goal, which would in fact be even more ambitious than their current demands.

When I landed in Edinburgh I went straight into my office and rang Richard.

'You wanted to know what I think we should do next?' I said. 'We should list the business. We can start now and get it done early. It will solve everything.'

Richard was thoughtful. I could hear that over the phone and over the miles. 'Give me 24 hours to think about it,' he said.

The next day Richard called me. 'Okay,' he said, 'you're on. Let's do it.'

A few hours later I got a call from Wilbur Ross.

'I hear you've decided to get on with the listing?' he said. 'That's terrific. Let me know how I can help.'

Both of my shareholders were completely on side. Now all I had to do was to get the executive team behind me. And list the business.

Payback Time

As part of our preparations to list Virgin Money, we decided it was time to repay the government the £150 million of debt that they had provided when we bought Northern Rock.

Once the terms had been agreed, the Chancellor, George Osborne, announced that he would like to come to the former Northern Rock offices in Newcastle to see the progress Virgin Money had made, and to meet the staff.

The date was set for 25 July 2014 and, given the profile and importance of the visit, we knew we needed to be better prepared than ever – and we tend to prepare for these things well.

The Chancellor was to arrive very early in the morning and wanted to visit a branch first thing, before coming into the main offices.

The trouble was that, for security reasons, we could not tell anyone who was coming.

Caroline had the facilities team give our famous Northumberland Street branch a lick of paint and asked the whole branch team to be in before seven o'clock in the morning – looking ship-shape – on the pretext that I was going to see them.

I am pleased to say that the team there did not think me enough of a princess for all that fuss – so they guessed that someone more important was coming, even though they did not know who.

I met the Chancellor around the corner from our branch very early in the morning and took him in to introduce him to the team there who showed him around.

After that we all sat down together for a cup of tea and a chat. I was surprised at how personable George Osborne was in the flesh. But not as surprised as when one of the Virgin Money team, Paul Bunyan, piped up: 'Hello, Chancellor, it's a real pleasure to meet you. I'm a Tory.'

I think it is fair to say that, in a staunch Labour heartland, George Osborne was pleased to meet a kindred spirit. He asked Paul – and the others – how long they had been with the business and if they had been there during the 'run' on Northern Rock.

Almost everyone, including Paul, had experienced those dark days. Paul told a story of how difficult those times had been – for him and for many others.

First, there had been the customer difficulties to deal with – but then, of course, everyone was worried about their job.

Paul had hoped to get married and his fiancée had wanted to go to university and study further – but none of that was possible during the crisis and subsequent nationalisation. But, since Virgin

Money had bought Northern Rock, the two had married and Paul's wife had been able to take up her studies.

It was a powerful story which we all enjoyed – and Paul, who is so interested in politics, enjoyed telling it to the Chancellor.

In return, the Chancellor asked Paul to go and tell his story at that year's Conservative Party conference. Paul was delighted, and did a brilliant job. He wrote to me afterwards and said, 'Some people dream of running out at Old Trafford. I'd always dreamt of making a speech at Conference. Thanks for making my dream come true.'

Back in Head Office that morning, Caroline had arranged for hundreds of staff to get together on the street to meet an important guest.

Everyone knew it was someone important because many people had been asked to come in earlier than their shift, and there was a lot of excitement and expectation building.

The Chancellor and I arrived quietly at a side door of the offices and no one saw us as we were taken to a small room on the ground floor of the building which, some years before, had housed the exclusive offices of the Northern Rock executive team.

Caroline came in. 'We have a problem,' she said. 'People think that the surprise guest is Cheryl Cole.'

My heart sank. With that sort of expectation, what would they think when George Osborne appeared?

So I asked one of my team, our COO, Mark Parker, to tell the hundreds of people gathered expectantly who our guest was, so that they were prepared when we arrived.

The Chancellor and I waited in the wings while Mark made his announcement. I must admit that I was surprised when, as soon as he said that the Chancellor was here to thank everyone for saving Northern Rock, a huge, spontaneous cheer went up. People were absolutely delighted that someone so important and so famous had made the trip to see them and to thank them.

As he walked up to our makeshift stage, phones and cameras were flashing. It was a great moment.

And then the Chancellor gave a speech.

He reminded everyone of the dark days of the past. And praised everyone for where they had got to now, and thanked us for repaying the £150 million of government debt.

You could have heard a pin drop. Some people were in tears.

It was a very special moment for many, many people whose lives, like that of Paul Bunyan, had been put on hold through the nationalisation of Northern Rock and the uncertainty of what might come next.

After his speech, the Chancellor went to our mortgage processing operation where the TV cameras had gathered for him to give his quarterly economic update.

Soon it was time for him to leave.

Caroline and I had wanted to give him a gift – although gifts to politicians can't be expensive. But we had acquired some historic memorabilia with Northern Rock. I especially liked some little tin money boxes – probably from the 1950s – with the Northern Rock brand enamelled on them.

We packed one beautifully in a big red (of course) gift box. It can't have been worth £5. But the Chancellor loved it and said that he would keep it on his desk at Number 11.

I hope he did. Maybe it sat next to that pack of Political Top Trumps.

Prices and Rockets

In the meantime, we were setting about listing the business.

It was an enormous effort to get the process off the ground. Lee, always cautious, was especially worried about the amount of work that needed to be done in a short space of time. And the timescales were tight, for sure.

It was May 2014 when I came back from Necker Island, and we felt that we had to list in October if we were to be successful, before Christmas set in.

Initially, I pulled together a small team of people – in particular Sophie Chandauka to get the Prospectus fit for purpose, and Paul Lloyd to get the Analysts' Presentation written and ready for market – who reported to my team.

We knew that we would need considerable support from the big investment banks and we saw a whole range of candidates, many of whom told us how difficult it is to list a business and all of whom put a wide range of valuations on our shares once they would be trading in the market.

We spent many hours on this required 'beauty parade' of banks. We finally decided to appoint Bank of America, whose team had done a fabulous presentation that showed they really understood us, and Goldman Sachs, whose team were outstanding and with whom we discovered, to my surprise, we could also have a good laugh!

As always, Allen & Overy were our lawyers because I always value the down-to-earth, honest and blunt advice of the excellent Andrew Ballheimer.

By now, momentum was gathering in the business. Dave was knuckling down to write the business review; Lee was doing the same with the financial reporting; Marian was keeping the regulators up to speed and, on the advice of Andrew Ballheimer, we appointed Andrew Emuss as our General Counsel.

Andrew replaced the wonderful Stephen Pearson in the General Counsel role – although Stephen had happily agreed to continue with us in an advisory role.

Stephen and I had first met at RBS, and I was delighted when he joined Virgin Money and shared his wealth of experience with us.

With Mark Carney
and Harriet Baldwin
launching the
Women in Finance
Charter at the Bank
of England, 2016.

With Norman
McLuskie in 2012 –
a supporter for
many years.

On Necker Island with Ash and Amy, 2015.

Some of the old team back together again in 2015. Clockwise from left: Dave Dyer, Mike Peckham, Roland Russell, Caroline Marsh, Rob Tarbuck, me, Paul Lloyd, Kevin Revell, Simon Leeming.

Opening the new
Virgin Money store
in Gosforth, 2013.

Listing on the London
Stock Exchange, 2014.

Before the marathon, and after, with
my wonderful supporters, 2015.

George Osborne's visit to our office in Gosforth, 2014.

Launching the new Virgin Money Australia business in 2010, with Matt Baxby.

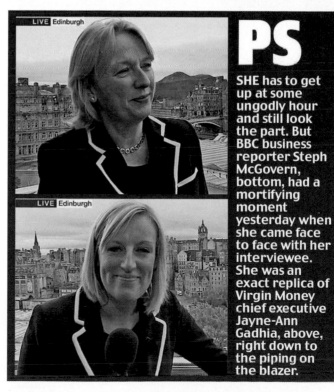

The morning of the 2014 Necker trip started off with an outfit challenge!

LIVE Edinburgh

LIVE Edinburgh

PS

SHE has to get up at some ungodly hour and still look the part. But BBC business reporter Steph McGovern, bottom, had a mortifying moment yesterday when she came face to face with her interviewee. She was an exact replica of Virgin Money chief executive Jayne-Ann Gadhia, above, right down to the piping on the blazer.

There are worse places to have a business meeting! The Temple at Necker Island.

The team together for our launch on the Stock exchange in 2014. From L-R: Andrew Emuss, Dave Dyer, Matt Elliot, Caroline Marsh, Lee Rochford, me, Mark Parker, Brian Brodie, Marian Martin, Anth Mooney, Darryl Evans, Michele Greene.

Interviewing Richard in front of the Gosforth team, 2013.

EBO (Everyone's Better Off) stars of the month celebration, March 2014.
L-R: Jason Clarkson, Craig Barron, me, Sinead Clarke, Dave Walker, Jim Starling.

Reflections of Sir Brian Pitman, 2007.

Our last family picture. Ash, Amy, me, Mum and Dad, 2015.

He had been through a lot since the financial crisis, including advising the Royal Bank and Fred Goodwin on their respective legal positions along the way.

But, after a particularly difficult Board in March 2014, Stephen had been sitting opposite me in our London office and I could see that the pupil in his left eye was as tiny as a pinhead.

He shrugged it off, but that weekend he rang me from hospital in Suffolk, having suffered a slight stroke. The pressures from the Board were starting to show, for sure.

So the successful float of Virgin Money had become important for more than just business reasons: we wanted to broaden our shareholder base and build a new Board ready for life as a listed business.

The trouble was that I had, for the first (and, so far, the last) time in my life, booked a three-week holiday. We were off to the Caribbean, first with our niece, Georgina, and then with our favourite family of five – the Bells.

The problem was that I couldn't cancel my holiday and stay married.

So the Prospectus and the Analysts' Presentation were just going to have to be written on holiday. And as a result, Paul came too.

We stayed in a villa on the island and Paul stayed in a nearby hotel. I would get up at 3.20 a.m. every morning to meet Paul so we could work till 9 a.m., by which time everyone else was up and about.

Paul would then work in the morning and we would meet again in the afternoon to move things forward while the UK team was awake.

We always managed dinner together, but other than that I don't think Paul saw much of the Caribbean sunshine. Thanks to his sacrifice and diligence, not to mention the tolerance of his wife, at home looking after the children, we went home with all of the paperwork largely complete.

Before the holiday, and before we had committed pen to paper, I had been on the road for some weeks with our bankers, meeting investors and telling the Virgin Money story so that we could be confident that there was enough interest to list the business. It was clear that there was.

But interest is one thing. To get a valuation and a share price on listing day, an enormous amount of detailed legal work is essential, and it all needs to be supported by analysis from market experts. These were the people whom I had once heard called 'City scribblers', but this description was demeaning – they all seemed pretty clever to me.

We knew we needed to put our best foot forward as we presented to them.

We decided to take them to the erstwhile Northern Rock offices in Gosforth to show them the scale and potential of Virgin Money, to take them around our operations, to let them meet our people, and then to present our story.

Caroline had been brilliant as ever and a spare floor in the building was turned into our version of an auditorium.

The night before, we had dinner with the banks and the analysts in the Great Hall of Jesmond Dene House hotel. It felt like an important moment as we began the process to list Virgin Money in the very place where Northern Rock had come to such a grinding halt, resulting in its de-listing from the stock market only six years earlier.

The presentation went well, despite our nerves, and now we were ready to go on the road and see again those investors who had expressed an interest in Virgin Money and to tell them our detailed plans for the future. We went to lots of investor meetings in the US and across Europe.

Lee and I did the presentations. Dave provided vital back-up, including music and a joke book to keep us going, and Mike Peckham came, ostensibly to manage the complex logistics, but also to keep the peace. It was a proper road trip!

But during the process it was announced that the Bank of England was planning shortly to announce an important new capital requirement for banks. The leverage ratio was to be a new measure for European banks to ensure that capital was sufficient to protect customers, and every institution was waiting to see how it affected them.

We could not list with confidence without knowing what capital we were required to hold, in case it affected the listing price.

So, unusually, we delayed our listing date until we had clarity on the capital requirement. Within days the number came through. We had been right to wait, and we had plenty of capital. Now we were ready to go. It was 31 October 2014.

That morning I woke early in the Haymarket Hotel in London to a call from Patrick McCall – one of the Virgin directors on my Board and a long-time friend and colleague.

He was in contact with the team in the Mojave Desert, where Virgin Galactic were about to undertake their first major test flight with the rocket decoupling from the mother ship.

'Sorry I can't be at the meeting today,' said Patrick. 'But I'll be ringing in and so will the other Virgin guys. I know it's a big day for you – getting ready for listing – and we wouldn't miss it for the world.'

We chatted for a while about how amazing it was that Virgin Money was about to list on the stock market after everything we had been through.

And I reminded Patrick that, when I had first met Richard Branson all those years ago in Holland Park, he was already talking about taking people into space and that I had thought it an exciting pipe dream – nothing more. But now, this too was to be realised – and all on the same day.

That day was frantic in our London offices. Calls were made. Bankers rushed in and out. The 'i's were dotted and 't's were crossed on the Listing Prospectus. The Board met and signed off risk statements and market disclosures.

As the evening drew in, the Board met to approve the next and final step in the listing process.

It was a dark night as the Board, the Virgin Money executive team, bankers and lawyers – and all such others as seem to be needed for such events – gathered in the boardroom at our London offices in Eagle Place.

The Virgin guys joined over the telephone. The meeting started and soon we were discussing stock market pricing. Before too long, the Virgin guys started to drop off the phone call, one by one.

To start with, I thought they didn't like the direction of the pricing discussions and were corralling together to see what they could do about it.

But then my phone rang on silent. It was Patrick.

I left the boardroom to take the call so fast that, having kicked off my shoes under the table, as I often do, I didn't have time to put them on again.

In stockinged feet, I hurried into the reception area of our London offices. A little Virgin train was whizzing around the ceiling as it does on the hour every hour.

'What's up?' I asked Patrick.

'The spaceship's crashed,' he said.

Going Public

The weekend after the Galactic crash was a bleak one.

First and foremost, a pilot had died in the accident and another was seriously injured, and we were all devastated about that.

As soon as he heard about it, Richard had headed straight out to the Mojave Desert to be with the team. The people there, led by George Whitesides, had devoted years of their lives to get to this point and we were all heartbroken for them.

But the Virgin spirit soon kicked in and everyone determined to pick themselves up, understand what had happened – and to start again.

Of course, the accident made headlines worldwide, and everyone was talking about it. I remember taking Amy to school the next morning, and all of the parents were keen to hear for themselves what had happened.

Over the weekend we hunkered down to think hard about what to do with the listing. Should we press ahead in the face of the media coverage? Was it disrespectful if we did?

On the Tuesday following the crash, Richard Branson rang me. 'I'm just back from Mojave. They are pushing on with things – and so should you.'

So we were off again.

We were ready to float the business. All that remained was to agree the price at which investors would buy in. The banks did a huge amount of work to build a list of interested investors, and on the evening of 12 November we gathered in a too-small room in Goldman Sachs's offices in Fleet Street to discuss the list of potential investor names – and the price.

There was a lot of interest in the business and there was plenty of demand for our shares. Our aim was to list at a price of around £3 per share.

After much discussion, as we built the first share register of top-notch investors, we agreed a listing price of £2.83 per share and headed off to Allen & Overy's offices in London's Bishopsgate for the formal Board meeting that would conclude the formalities of the deal.

On the way there, Richard Branson called me. 'Well done,' he said. 'We all wanted the price to be around £3, and it's close enough.

Well done for getting this done so fast and so well. Here's to a new future for Virgin Money.'

But the Board meeting was far less positive. As always, the Board had wanted more!

Those of us who had worked almost 24/7 to get the business listed against all the odds felt the criticism sharply, and I could not stop myself from reacting.

'Everyone in this room – bankers, lawyers and executive team – have sacrificed everything to get to this point,' I said. 'I couldn't have wished for more from anyone. It is an amazing achievement and one that we should all be very proud of.'

You could have heard a pin drop. Some directors were avoiding eye contact by fiddling with their phones.

The atmosphere was tense as we agreed the final legal documents and started to sign the many pages of technical papers to commit the business to the markets.

As we were signing, someone opened a bottle of champagne. I couldn't drink it. The moment for celebration had been lost.

That night Caroline, Lee, Marian and I went back to the hotel. We had just successfully listed the business that we had acquired less than three years earlier and which, at that time, was on the ropes, fighting for its life and losing £120 million a year.

The next day, we were to appear at the London Stock Exchange to open the market and to see our shares trade for the first time.

I didn't really want to go to such a public event. I wanted quietly to celebrate with the people who had spent so many months doing nothing but getting the business ready for listing. Weekends sacrificed. Relationships strained. Work–life balance a bad joke.

But next morning we all arrived at the Stock Exchange and were taken to a side room where husbands and wives, as well as bankers and lawyers, had gathered to congratulate us.

I wanted no speeches. Getting to this point had been tough and tense at times. We did not need speeches congratulating us and suggesting that it had been a bed of roses.

In the side room there is a beautiful book in which a new listing is registered, as well as historical artefacts of previous listings over the many years of Stock Exchange history.

Champagne and Buck's Fizz were available, next to some delicious, plump pastries. It should have been a great morning.

But Caroline had the task of orchestrating the morning and, when she suggested to our Chairman that no speeches were required, she was subject to a response that left her in tears.

It seemed that speeches were required after all. So we made them.

Then we all stepped out onto the balcony of the Stock Exchange as the market opened. I was given an engraved glass tablet that would act as a key to open the market.

I placed the tablet on the podium and the Stock Exchange screens welcomed Virgin Money to the market. We had made it.

The company that had started twenty years earlier in a small building in Norwich with £4 million of capital had bought Northern Rock, the poster-child of the financial crisis, turned it round and listed it at a total value of £1.25 billion.

It had been one hell of a journey.

The Extra Mile

Each year we have sponsored the London Marathon we have invited our friends and families to join the Virgin Money team at the grandstand at the finishing line.

It is halfway down the Mall, draped with Union flags and full of noise, colour and emotion as athletes and fun runners – and everyone in between – drag themselves over the finishing line to relief and celebration.

Every year one organisation is chosen to be the London Marathon's appointed charity. It is a great opportunity for these charities to raise a lot of money, as so many runners are sponsored to run for them.

In 2015 our chosen charity was to be Cancer Research UK, which is led by the wonderful, inspirational and brilliant Sir Harpal Kumar. So we invited Harpal and his team to join us at the finishing line to watch the 2014 marathon. It was as inspirational as ever.

To add to the emotion, we at Virgin Money had, in 2013, sponsored a group of wounded soldiers to walk to the South Pole and, not least because Prince Harry was with them, their exploits were made into a fascinating documentary.

When they got back from that adventure, almost all of the soldiers wanted to run the London Marathon, and Harpal and I watched as they came over the finishing line – some with prosthetic limbs, others having lost their sight.

'If they can do it – don't you think we can too?' asked Harpal, and, carried away by the events of the day, I agreed.

Ash was more sensible. 'You can do it, but only if Mike runs with you,' he said.

Mike has been a friend and colleague for many years. An ex-soldier himself, he still runs the training school I attended as part of the Leadership Challange. If you're with him, you feel you're going to be okay.

Mike was at the finishing line too and was happy to agree. So, there and then, I made the commitment. And it was impossible to go back on it.

For the next few months the focus was on signing up a team to run, too. We thought that a team of senior bankers would raise a lot of money and I wrote to them all asking them to join me.

It is amazing how many bankers have bad backs. Or dodgy knees. Or insufficient time.

But a few agreed to join and to run for Cancer Research UK and, specifically, for the Crick Institute, which, supported by Cancer Research and a number of other partners, was destined to become the biggest biomedical research laboratory in Europe.

Antony Jenkins, then CEO of Barclays, signed up. Anthony Gutman from Goldman Sachs did too. Peter Johnson from Travelex was keen to beat his personal best of just over three hours. And Mark Carney, Governor of the Bank of England, also agreed to run. With me and Harpal, we had a team of six runners, and I knew then that I had better get myself sorted out.

Richard Branson was my first, and most generous, sponsor. He had always teased me that I should do it, having completed the marathon himself in 2010, in a fetching pair of fairy wings.

But I don't think Richard ever really thought I would agree to do it – I'm not exactly built as a runner.

The sponsorship grew. People were generous and confident that I would do it, so I had to. But how on earth could I find the time alongside listing the business, running the company – and being a mum?

And it was then that I realised that, like everything I had managed to achieve this far, I was not going to manage this on my own.

Mike runs a charity called 'Hire a Hero' which supports military personnel who leave the Army and who are looking for a civilian job. In 2014 I needed someone to cover maternity leave and to run my office, and Mike had sent three ex-Army officers to meet me.

In the end we employed all three and Ross Boyd took on the challenge of running my office and, to some extent, my life. He had done three tours of duty in Afghanistan and was keen to learn the ropes in Civvy Street – as well as to support me and Virgin Money to the very best of his ability.

He was pleased that one way he could support me immediately was to go running with me, and one dark, wet, cold December night we started out by running home from our Edinburgh offices.

It was so wet that I thought people were throwing buckets of water at me. And the run from the office to my house in Edinburgh felt like a marathon itself – although it is actually less than 2.5 miles. I was absolutely sure that I had no chance of running 26.2 miles.

At the same time, my friend and trainer, Colin Wycherley, stepped forward. I had met Colin at the local gym a few years earlier and he had helped me to keep fit since then. He took my marathon commitment seriously and started to put together a plan.

The day after I had struggled home with Ross, Colin met me for our first training run together. It was six agonising miles. I hated every minute of it.

But, between Ross and Colin, they got me running nearly every day for months.

On Saturdays they would turn up at my house at 4 a.m. (yes, 4 a.m.) so that we could all go on a long run together. Starting then meant that, even for the long runs at my speed, we could be home for breakfast with our respective families.

We ran every Saturday morning through the winter. It was cold, dark, wet, windy and miserable. But we had a laugh. Well, Ross and Colin did, at least!

We talked for hours about everything you can imagine.

We ran through the city. Through the country. Over the Forth Road Bridge. Ash would meet us – miles away – with coffee and bacon sandwiches, and drive us home. I couldn't get out of the car afterwards because every bit of me hurt.

When I was in London, Ross would run with me at 5 a.m. in the mornings by the river and we would discuss the Army, the family, the world and the business.

Mike would arrive from time to time and we would do the same.

Eventually I succeeded in running the required eighteen miles needed for you to know, apparently, that you can run a marathon. There were two weeks to go and the talk turned to 'tapering'. That's when you are allowed to run less and eat more. My favourite time.

And then the weekend itself approached. I don't mind admitting that I was terrified. Ash, Amy and my mum and dad all went down to London on the Friday, and we went to the Palladium to see *Cats* on the Saturday afternoon.

That night, Ash and I left Amy with mum and dad in the hotel and went out to the Spaghetti House restaurant for dinner. It was like the condemned man's last meal.

Next to us sat a man on his own. He had trainers on, and his race timing tag was already attached. The three of us talked running and marathons and I couldn't really believe that I would be part of it the next day.

When Ash and I were on our own, I made sure that he knew about my life insurance cover. I genuinely thought that it was possible that I might not get out of this one alive!

Later that evening I went to the Tower Hotel where all the runners and the sponsors gather. Mike and Ross and I were all staying there so we could get bussed to the start line at Greenwich the next morning with the elite athletes.

We met briefly and agreed our plan for the morning. My room was on the seventh floor so we agreed to meet early before the lifts were clogged up with everyone coming down at the same time.

When I got to my room I discovered that the London Marathon team had sent me new kit to run in. I'm afraid I stuck to the old tatty stuff.

I left the curtains open and enjoyed the lovely view of Tower Bridge and contemplated the madness that had got me here.

Surprisingly, I slept well and woke to literally hundreds of good luck messages. I was the first of our group to get down for breakfast.

The elite athletes were all there. Small, wiry, focused, and eating huge amounts. Then Mike and Ross arrived. Everyone ate a lot – but I have never seen Mike, who eats sparsely, pack away so much.

And then we were off to join the athletes and celebs waiting for the bus to the start line. Jenson Button was there, and Chris Evans.

I was also looking out for the Lord Provost of Edinburgh, who had agreed to run with me. I had met Donald Wilson at an official event where he was wearing his wonderful, diamond-encrusted chain of office, which I had admired. I wondered if he might be running with it on!

And suddenly there he was, in a T-shirt with the chain Photoshopped on to it! It said everything about the fun and the spirit of the London Marathon.

Everyone was nervous.

We walked together out of the Tower Hotel and to the bridge, where two old red London buses were waiting. They were the old Routemasters, with rough seats and a wire across the roof from front to back that used to be tweaked to ring the bell.

Soon we were off. A motley crew of athletes, celebrities, decent runners and the just plain terrified.

I sat next to Mike and can't remember a word we said to each other. It was raining. Some people – clearly mad – were running to the start line.

And then we arrived.

We got out of the bus and reached the Virgin Money tent at the start. It was wet and cold but had the benefit of having its own set of Portaloos.

Anthony Gutman was there wearing a brown silk number from an Asian airline. He only needed a cigarette in a long holder to look like a James Bond villain.

Then Colin arrived. His wife, Gemma, was also running so they had stayed, separately to us, near the start line.

Then there was Antony Jenkins, in a blue rain poncho, and the rest of the team and all the Virgin Money staff runners, and friends and families. People were stretching out on the wet grass. My friend Sue – my age but fitter and faster – arrived too.

Soon we were outside waiting for the starting gun. And then, without much fanfare, we were off.

Mike ran next to me, and for some reason started chatting to an older man next to him. It turned out that they both came from Chepstow and recognised each other from the running club.

I nearly died with laughter when the older man asked Mike, 'Are you good for age too?' Mike and his wife Lizzie had run 100 miles together the previous year to celebrate their fiftieth birthdays. It had taken them about twenty-two hours. I'd call that pretty good for his age.

It turned out that Ross and Colin had learned jokes to tell on the way. I soon put a stop to that. It just wasn't a laughing matter.

The crowds were truly amazing. The costumes even more so, although I winced every time I ran behind a bloke in nothing more than a G-string.

A team of men ran carrying an enormous rowing boat. Goodness knows why. And I couldn't work out why we kept being overtaken by a dinosaur. Surely I wasn't overtaking them back? But when I finished it turned out there had been thirty-six of them on the course.

Ash, Amy and Ross's wife, Sazzy, as well as Sue's husband and daughter, Nichol and Lucy, and our friend Dave Crossman, tracked us down and cheered us on at certain points round the course. It was good to see them.

Sooner than I expected we were back at Tower Bridge and at the halfway mark. It had taken me less than the 2 hours 50 minutes I'd planned. It felt good, and Ross and I took a selfie on the bridge to celebrate.

Then we had to turn right, through Canary Wharf for the second half.

It was absolute hell.

Once we got to eighteen miles, I couldn't get out of my mind that I'd never run further than this before. And I still had 8.2 agonising miles to go. I began to feel that I just couldn't do it. And that's a bad place to be mentally, that's for sure.

'Have we got any bananas?' I asked Mike.

'Let me look in the cupboard,' he said sarcastically, opening his running jacket. 'No, we have no bananas.'

I turned to speak with Colin and didn't notice that Mike was gone for a while until he returned with, you've guessed it, a bunch of bananas.

'Where did you get them from?' I asked.

'I popped to Tesco's,' he said.

Of course he did. In the middle of the bloody London Marathon.

I ate a banana and pretended to feel better.

And then, just as I was at the end of my tether, and completely by surprise, one of my oldest and best friends stepped out of the crowd and gave me a hug. 'Don't you give up now,' she said. 'You've come too far.'

It was like a gift from God. As was the Vaseline that miraculously appeared, as my short sleeves rubbed my arms until they bled.

Ash and Amy were waiting as we came back on to the Embankment, and then it didn't seem so far after all.

We had stuck together all the way round – Ross running backwards and forwards and eating pounds of free jelly babies from the crowd – just to stop his boredom.

Soon we were at the Houses of Parliament and still the crowds were urging us on.

Down by St James's Park – and there was Buckingham Palace – flag flying. Turn right. Up the Mall.

There's the end.

To my surprise – and to everyone else's – I stepped on the gas and fairly sprinted up the Mall.

In the Virgin Money tent by the finishing line, there were my friends, colleagues and family. There was my mum – and my dad, cheering and waving his walking stick.

And at the very end, over the line, Nick Bitel, Chief Executive of London Marathon Events, was waiting with my medal and a bunch of flowers. 'Thank God we haven't killed you,' he said.

And there were Ash and Amy – beaming to see me arrive in one piece. I'd made it.

And the only reason I did was because of all the support, the sacrifice and the care I got from others.

Just like my entire journey, really. So many people have been there and supported me every step of the way.

Women in Finance

Every June for many decades, the Chancellor of the Exchequer has given a speech at Mansion House in London. The Governor of the Bank of England and the Lord Mayor of London are the esteemed guests, and the room is full of the great and the good of the City.

Mansion House is a wonderful setting and has been the home of the Lord Mayor for centuries. Once you are through security, you climb a set of carpeted stairs and admire the paintings on the way up as you queue to be formally announced. Then you enter an enormous reception room, and are introduced to the Lord Mayor and their partner.

The reception room is exceptional and a real treat for a historian like me. It seats hundreds of people and has a balcony overlooking the enormous, elaborate and ornate dining room. Diners sit at the many tables that adjoin the long top table along the back wall.

I like to remember that Chancellors such as Gladstone and Churchill held dinners and gave speeches here – during war and peace – and in the service of many monarchs through the ages.

Because so many people attend, the seating plan is complex. As you arrive you are handed a long concertina of a document, in which guests are listed alphabetically with a table reference. You then find your table and your particular seat on the plan.

The tables are dressed beautifully with gleaming antique silver and gold, candles and flowers, and the food is served on beautiful china and in sparkling crystal glasses.

I have had the privilege of attending the dinner for a number of years now and have sat on many different tables – near and far from the centre.

In June 2015 I arrived early for dinner and looked around for a friendly face. The evening is a very male-dominated affair and it is often hard to work out who's who, with all the men dressed identically in black tie and dinner suits.

So I was pleased to see António Horta-Osório – the CEO of Lloyds Bank – in a side room off the main reception area and went to say hello to him.

Not long after, another banker joined us. Eventually, António was engrossed in another conversation.

The other banker turned to me. 'Where are you sitting?' he asked.

I admitted that I didn't know, as I had not yet taken my glasses out of my bag – I can assure you that almost everyone needs glasses to read their name on this plan.

Now, this was a man who had always been aloof with me. That may have been because I am a woman in what is very much a man's world. It might be because Virgin is seen as a small player, as a 'challenger' bank. Or it might be because I am not as polished as most bankers.

But at that point his own polish faded.

He pulled open his seating plan, and found my name. 'You're on the top table,' he announced.

He turned the page over and his finger swept across the table names.

'Fuck! You're sat next to the Chancellor!' he exclaimed in astonishment.

I was astonished, too, but I like to think I acted cool, or as cool as you can be in that kind of environment. And I enjoyed his surprise enormously – even though I hope I didn't show it!

Dinner sat next to the Chancellor was memorable. We talked about the history of the place and his predecessors, how government works and the relatively limited data available to Chancellors, upon which to make decisions.

As he stood up to speak he whispered, 'The cameras will be on you. Don't forget to look interested!' His speech was about the future of RBS, which of course interested me in any case, not least because I had worked there.

I always found George Osborne much more human in real life than the press ever portrayed him. And part of that humanity was his commitment to improving gender equality in society and in business, and especially in financial services.

The following month one of his team asked me if I would be prepared to undertake a review into why women make less progress in financial services than in other industries. The 'Women in Finance' review and consequent 'Empowering Productivity: Harnessing the Talents of Women in Financial Services' report were to form part of the Productivity Plan aimed at improving UK productivity, which continues to lag behind many other developed countries.

I was pleased to be asked but slightly dubious about the task.

I had never wanted to be seen as a radical feminist. Ash and I had both wanted to succeed on our own merits and not be part of any programme of positive discrimination.

But what intrigued me was that the data showed that the financial services industry was so much worse than elsewhere. Why on earth should that be the case? And had it contributed to the financial crisis that had caused so much misery for so many people?

I decided to accept, get involved and undertake the review.

The problem was that there had been so many other, similar reviews and I did not want mine just to add to the pile. I wanted it to have teeth. And I wanted it to be based on what women – and men – really said, rather than what we thought they might say.

So, with the blessing of my Board, I put together a small team to investigate further. Mike agreed to play a leading organisational role, and Emily Cox and Jay Sheth committed to a huge review programme.

We started by surveying people who worked in financial services companies across the UK. About 3,500 people contributed to the survey – 20 per cent of them men.

And I was fascinated to see that the issue holding women back in financial services is one thing and one thing only.

Culture.

The old boys' network persists and tends to recruit in its own image.

There is an expectation that 'good people' will be 'present' – in other words, long hours are demanded – especially in investment banks.

Women tend not to like arguing for their annual bonus – a regular ritual in financial services companies – and feel that men tend to shout the loudest and therefore get paid the most.

Our respondents proposed sensible solutions – to train line managers to avoid inevitable unconscious bias – and to use the technologies of today to support more flexible working conditions.

The review was owned and supported in Her Majesty's Treasury by the Economic Secretary to the Treasury, Harriett Baldwin, and her team. They invited us to present our interim findings at Number 11 Downing Street on 4 November 2015.

By October we had the data and Mike, Emily and I agreed to meet to work out what to do with it.

We decided to spend an hour or two over dinner so we could discuss it properly, and so we booked a nice restaurant just off Marsham Street in London.

When we turned up, the place was heaving. There was a leaving party on and that, plus all the people normally there, meant that we could not hear each other speak.

The pub opposite was equally loud with football on the telly and a crowd watching it.

So we walked around the corner to the Astral Café where London cabbies stop for breakfast, lunch and dinner. The food is great. Take away or inside. Bottles of sauce on the tables. Huge helpings. Emily and I each had an enormous chilli con carne and a glass of unnamed wine. Mike had fish and chips.

The Formica table was too small for us to spread out papers – so we just talked.

And in the chilly, basic, friendly café with the tasty, home-cooked food, we discussed the way ahead for the Women in Finance review.

We decided that this was a business issue. Despite what people would have us believe, motherhood and child care were not major points. The issues of culture were solvable. But they needed focus.

Just like any other business problem.

So we decided to recommend that they should be addressed like any other business problem. That meant each business should have its own strategy and targets for gender inclusion, publish them and be prepared to be rewarded on them.

Simple.

When we arrived for our interim update at Number 11 we had the proposals presented rather more professionally than we had on the night of the taxi café. But the essence was the same.

The big meeting room on the first floor of Number 11 was full. Everyone was excited to be there.

The key issue was one of targets – and remuneration. We had recommended that executives in financial services companies should have their bonuses linked to achieving gender targets, so the tension was high.

One person from a US investment bank suggested that this was not fair as, she said, 'there are certain jobs in our business that are just not suitable for most women'.

We passed over that until one woman in the audience – shocked – brought us back to it.

'What job in your investment bank isn't suitable for a woman?' she asked.

'IT,' came the reply.

There was a gasp around the room. In an age when women can fight in the infantry that just cannot be right.

But the meeting created interest and engagement.

That night, a prominent banker invited me out to dinner and asked how he could improve the gender mix in his firm.

I was touched – and pleased. If *he* was positively engaged then we had achieved something. Then other companies, other women and other men engaged too. They wanted to know how they could help.

Encouraged by so much support, we pushed on to the final report which was due towards the end of February 2016, by which time we had met literally hundreds of leaders in financial services across the country. The challenge, commitment, engagement and support were inspiring.

When I spoke to Mark Carney, the Governor of the Bank of England, he was equally supportive and asked if there was anything he could do to help.

I asked if we could launch the review in the Court of the Bank of England and, to my delight, he agreed.

So, on 22 March 2016, I arrived at the Bank of England with Harriett Baldwin, our respective teams and a full house *in situ* ready to hear the final recommendations.

Before the formal proceedings, Harriett and I were invited to meet the Governor in his office. We sat at a large, leather-topped table and, before we left, I asked the Governor the history of the worn table-top.

'Every Governor of the Bank of England has worked at this table and in the very seat you are sitting,' he said.

It made me tingle to think of the decisions that had been made here. The crises discussed and avoided. Careers lost and found. Our futures depending on it.

We left the room for photographs and entered the magnificent Court of the Bank of England.

It is a huge, elegant room and, at one end, there is a historic piece of engineering.

When the British economy depended on shipping, Governors and their Court would be very focused on the safe arrival of vessels from overseas. They would look to the equipment, which would show them which way the wind was blowing, so that they would know when to expect a fully laden ship safely into port.

And that's where we get the expression from – 'let's see which way the wind is blowing'.

I didn't know that the Governor was going to make a full and supportive speech. But his contribution made sure that the review got properly picked up and seriously considered.

Her Majesty's Treasury adopted the recommendations as their own and published, on the same day, a Financial Services Charter to which companies were encouraged to sign up.

As I write, more than 100 financial services companies in the UK, employing over 500,000 people, have signed to commit to publishing their own gender targets and to driving equality in their businesses.

It is something that I hope will make a real difference to our profession, our people and our productivity.

At Virgin Money we have made our own commitment to achieving gender equality targets of fifty–fifty by 2020. It is not an easy ask, but I have yet to meet anyone in our business who does not want to help it happen.

The Public Eye

Having fought so hard to get the bank listed early, I worried a bit when Peter Norris, now Chairman of the Virgin Group, told me, 'Be careful what you wish for. I bet you'll hate the market scrutiny.'

As it turns out, nothing could be further from the truth.

I continue to love meeting the extremely clever and insightful banking analysts who write pages of analysis on Virgin Money.

In fact, I find it a continuing surprise that so many people, all around the world – in London, New York, Paris, Sydney and beyond – study the business we set up all those years ago and have a view on it. Some of those views are, in my opinion, right and others are not – but it is interesting and stimulating to see the business you set up, and which you have managed over so long, considered through a range of different lenses and from different points of view.

Dealing with investors is equally interesting. They all have different views and different comparison points. I prefer meeting those investors who invest for the long term and who want us to be sensible, solid and low risk. That matches my personality and our long-term view of the future of Virgin Money.

But it is also good to meet the hedge funds who buy and sell shares and take a more short-term view, managing to take advantage of both the ups and the downs of stock market movement. They are a good temperature check and help us to think about the specific market issues of the moment.

And, since we listed, there have been many such issues.

The first, only months after our market début, was the imposition of a new bank tax by the then Chancellor, George Osborne. Until that point, bank tax surcharges were paid only by the big banks, and the extension of the new tax to challengers like Virgin Money hit the share price hard.

Not long after, both government and regulators indicated their worries that the buy-to-let housing market might be overheating. We had no undue exposure to the market – but broadly the challenger sector did, and our share price came down again. It was a lesson to me to make sure that our unique position in the market is clearly understood by analysts, investors and the press alike.

But if, post-listing, managing the markets was a new challenge, managing the business internally had got much easier.

Glen Moreno, previously Chairman at Pearson and Senior Independent Director at Lloyds Bank, had joined as Deputy Chairman to take over, post-listing, as Chairman from Sir David Clementi.

Glen was positive, supportive, engaged and fun. He set about reviewing the Board and meeting as many people as he could in the business. He travelled to Edinburgh, Chester, Newcastle and Norwich – meeting people who had never seen a Chairman before – and making everyone feel great about what they had achieved and what was to come.

He changed the tone of the Board from one which saw its place as driving the commercial agenda to one which put risk management first. He moved attention from using remuneration to micro-manage the team to genuine incentivisation. He made sure that the shareholder directors were not part of the Board Committees.

Most importantly, he was clear that I should be able to choose my own team and replace those who were not going to contribute 100 per cent to the journey ahead.

As a result, he supported me in appointing Dave as our CFO – a move which was as transformational inside the business as was Glen's own appointment to the Board.

And so the business thrived with a happy, hard-working team, a supportive Board, a clear strategy and a continued mission to change the world by making everyone better off.

At its highest, Virgin Money's share price valued the business we had set up in 1995 for £4 million at almost £2 billion.

Then came 2016.

We had endured a difficult Christmas, with the whole family suffering from norovirus. My father had been diagnosed with cancer of the oesophagus. And, in February, with Ash and Amy away skiing, my mother said she was breathless. I took her to the doctors and then to A&E. She died three days later from pneumonia.

Meanwhile, David Cameron had announced the date of the EU referendum.

I was asked if I would join the Board of 'Stronger In' – the campaign group arguing for the UK to remain in the EU – led by Will Straw and Peter Mandelson.

With tough times at home and a business to run, I declined, but I did join the Board of 'Scotland Stronger In' as it was easier to juggle all my commitments north of the border.

It was an intense time.

On Monday 21 June, three days before the referendum vote, I was part of a small group that dined with David Cameron at Number 10 Downing Street. The mood was tired, but quietly positive.

On Thursday 23 June my father, who was by now dreadfully ill, insisted that we take him to vote. We had not got him a postal vote as, frankly, we did not think he would be here to use it. So, with huge difficulty, he went to the local polling station and cast his vote to remain in the EU. 'Because,' he said, 'it is right for Amy.'

That night I stayed up all night, and, along with so many others, felt a real sense of shock at the outcome of the vote.

All of the Virgin Money executive team gathered in our Edinburgh offices at 5 a.m. on the morning of 24 June to work out how it would affect us and what we should do next.

We had a widescreen TV in the boardroom.

As David Cameron came out of Downing Street and resigned, I could not believe that this was the man whom I had sat next to at dinner only four nights previously.

And, at that moment, our share price commenced a sharp, long fall, as markets worried about the impact of leaving the EU on the economy, on the airlines, on the banks and especially on the challenger banks.

That weekend was tough. I was worried about the vote, our country, our business.

And my dad was also fading fast. On the Saturday night he needed help even to move on his pillows, and on the Sunday we asked for a Marie Curie nurse to stay with us all to help.

On the Monday morning she said she felt he should be taken to the local hospice.

He didn't really want to go, and Ash and I wanted it to be his decision and his alone. He was, after all, entirely *compos mentis*. More so, I remember thinking, than most of our country and our politicians.

He decided that he would go into the hospice. I sat on his bed and held his hands, and fought back the tears. 'You've been strong through all of this,' he said. 'Be strong now.'

He refused to go in an ambulance, and somehow we got him into Ash's car and to the hospice – about four miles away from home.

He hated it. But we cheered him up by taking in cans of his favourite beer which, by that stage, was all he could swallow.

On the Wednesday night I went to see him, and then got the sleeper train down to London. There was the final meeting of David Cameron's Business Advisory Group, of which I was a member, at Number 10 that morning.

It was a sombre affair, enlivened slightly by the fact that Boris Johnson and Michael Gove were publicly at war with each other.

I sat next to the Prime Minister during the meeting and, as I shook his hand on the way out, I felt huge sadness at the events that had conspired to bring down this warm, caring, dutiful man who had sacrificed so much for his country.

I flew home and went straight to the hospice. Dad had taken a turn for the worse and, although he could still manage a sip of beer, he could barely speak. I sat at his bedside and told him about my trip to Downing Street.

'How's business?' he asked.

'Not great,' I said sadly.

'You'll be alright,' he said.

It was the last thing he said to me. He died that night and I was there to hold his hand.

And, of course, he was correct. We will be alright.

If the story of Virgin Money tells me nothing more, it's that it is the dark and difficult moments that make us. They define us. They create us. Because they compel us to succeed.

Now that the country has voted to leave the EU, we will make a success of it. It needs good people. Hard work. Exceptional leadership.

Vision and inspiration. The determination never to give up. If we can heal the divisions in our country and work together then we can create a new beginning. It will be alright.

That's what I've learned over all these years.

In the end, working together for a common purpose with good people is the only way to be successful.

Work hard and have fun. Strive always to make everyone better off.

In the end, it will be alright.

Chapter 7

THIS MUCH I HAVE LEARNED

Diversity Matters

THE CITY is a funny place.

Every day I meet clever, hardworking and decent people who do their jobs well. Lawyers, accountants, bankers and people who have worked in some of the biggest businesses all their lives and who have climbed the career ladder to success.

But it can be a closed world. Many sons follow fathers into careers, even today. Many City high-flyers have been to school together. Others have done great deals together and sometimes made each other rich.

And that, it seems to me, is why they make exceptions for each other from time to time.

When people do a bad job and leave a business, the truth behind their departure is, too often in my opinion, never made public. People worry that to tell the truth would leave a bad taste or bring the business into some sort of disrepute.

So we have people who move from job to job in the City, often having taken a year out on full pay, turning up again to do another mediocre job and to be moved on again, in hushed tones, to their next employer.

It sometimes seems as if the old boy network is still looking after its own.

I have tried to question this in the past and been given short shrift. When I asked a Chairman recently why he had employed someone without asking me for a reference first, he apologised for 'upsetting' me. It made me wonder if he would have behaved in the same way had I been a man.

It is the same sort of behaviour that, in my view, led to the financial crisis.

Of course, people in the City saw the emerging risks. To respond, if I may, to the Queen's question, 'Why did no one see the crisis coming?' – my answer is that some did. In my opinion, they just chose to do nothing about it, for fear of saying the wrong thing or being excluded from the network.

I encountered this with PPI. RBS knew it was a problem but did not raise it as they did not want to be the first to do so. It would have affected their share price.

Why did the ABN AMRO deal go ahead in the end? Was it really seen as economically sensible at the time of completion – or would there have been a loss of 'face' and fees if the acquirers had walked away?

It is for these reasons that I am such a huge supporter of diversity in the City.

The issues at the heart of the financial crisis seem to have been caused, in part at least, by the same faces having the same conversations and fearing to speak up and rock the boat despite us operating in a fast-changing world.

In recent months many people have asked me how, when there are so few women in senior roles in financial services, I seem to have bucked the trend.

Firstly, let's be clear: I might be quite unusual in banking, but there are very successful women throughout our society who run huge businesses. I am inspired by Carolyn McCall at easyJet, Alison Brittain at Whitbread and Liv Garfield at Severn Trent. Let's face it, we have our second female Prime Minister and little is made of her gender. There are many more examples of success.

Banking and insurance, however, seem to stand out as male bastions over the years and that has not been good for the stability of the system either before or during the crisis.

I think the reason for this must be that the major banks and insurers have been around for generations. They are traditional institutions run by traditional people. Like many institutions, some of them have been slow to change. Current management have tended to recruit in their own image, sometimes with conscious, but usually unconscious, biases.

One of the major benefits I have had is that Virgin has never been part of the Establishment and Virgin Money has never been a traditional institution. The very fact that it is a new banking brand with new ideas marks it out as different. It has given us permission to rock the boat and to look at things afresh.

In looking at things differently, you have to understand them first. Deeply. One of the benefits of running a small bank is that you see the whole business and have to get to grips with the innards of its workings. On more than one occasion, new employees who have joined us from big banks have remarked, 'This is just the same as the bank I came from – the complexities are the same – it just has less zeros.'

One particular benefit we have had is that, as a new bank, we do not have the legacy issues of the past to deal with, so we can focus on the culture and on the future. It has set us apart and enabled us to run the business well.

In doing new business in a new way, and doing it well and with purpose, I have never found any issues in being a woman in banking and have enjoyed liberal doses of support from influential men along the way. We all need that. No one can make it on their own.

I guess there have also been some personality traits that have made a difference too. Sheer bloody-mindedness has helped. Some men believe that makes me 'a difficult woman' and have told me so to my face. I have ignored them. I am driven to succeed, to make a difference and to prove a point. That means that when I am knocked down, I get up again. In the end, I have always felt that if you do what you believe is right, with integrity, you can't go far wrong. Once, RBS sent me for some psychological profiling by a firm of business consultants. To my surprise the man who gave me my feedback said, 'You are the bravest person we have met in business.' It took me aback but I get the point.

Be brave but don't be stupid. Take a risk but know what to do if it goes wrong. Know who your supporters are. Never give up. There is no doubt that it can be a challenge. But how much better if that challenging approach were to be welcomed and celebrated by a new City that represents the features of the society that we live in day to day?

I see signs of this new City everywhere.

First, I see it in the support for Her Majesty's Treasury's Women in Finance Charter. Over 100 organisations, employing over 500,000 UK staff, signed within the first year – pledging to increase the proportion of women in their workforce.

I think this will change the way that organisations think and act.

Some senior City leaders are embracing and encouraging this change, speak about it publicly and walk the walk. We need powerful leaders to drive this new City culture because they have real credibility to do so.

But they also know that diversity brings a safer and more profitable City – and one that is fit for our rapidly changing times. A new City is needed, I think, to build the new businesses of the future, to drive sustainable economic growth and to create a society where everyone can succeed.

We need real vision, energy and drive to make it happen and, in my view, that impulse needs to be nurtured today more than ever.

I would encourage the creation of an entrepreneurial City, operating with a growth mindset and which can build from, but break out of, the established ways of thinking and of doing things.

New businesses, I believe, will develop with diversity of workforce, challenge to tradition and creativity of thought. And we need men and women of all races, beliefs and capabilities to inspire that change.

Hoping and Coping

One of the changes that I believe could help business in general, and the City in particular, to grow and to flourish would be an openness to discuss and to deal with the mental health issues that dog many of us as human beings at some point in our lives.

That is why Virgin Money chose Heads Together, a charity which aims to de-stigmatise mental health issues in all walks of life, as the 2017 Virgin Money London Marathon Charity of the Year.

Without that encouragement I would never have considered writing about my own experiences.

But the truth is that, like so many people, I have lived with mental health issues for periods of my life.

My mother had a difficult childhood after the death of her own mother, suddenly, when my mum was only thirteen years old. As a result, her teenage years were turbulent. She left the family home with her sister and they soon got separated and sent to 'digs'. Some were happy and loving. Others less so. Indeed, one landlady attempted suicide on at least one occasion.

All of this affected my mother's mental health and I grew up in an environment where mum worried about her 'nerves' and managed them through a regular dosage of tranquillisers. Over the years, she conquered all this and came off the medication, gave up smoking and lived a happier and fuller life as a consequence.

But she never really got over the early loss of her mother and the impact that had on her own early life.

Of course, all of that had an impact on my own beginnings. I was an only child, awkward and much taller than any of my contemporaries. It is no surprise that I was bullied at school but I had to make the best of it as I didn't want to worry my mum with my own problems.

So I toughened up and worked out how to survive on my own. Some strong friendships. A fantasy world with the boy band of the day ... the Osmonds. And the stories.

I would go to bed and create all sorts of stories where, however badly I was faring, I would picture myself coming out on top. 'Jayne-Anne the fighter' would lead the underdog to triumph and I would feel great about it.

And throughout my life, whenever I am under huge stress, the stories come flooding back. They play in the background of my real life and oddly they make me better. They give me hope. And they help me cope.

I have found that, whatever life has thrown at me, the best thing always has been to work hard and find my purpose. Everything seems so much more worthwhile if you truly believe that your efforts will have some sort of positive and lasting effect on the world around you.

Which, of course, is easy to say but very much harder to do, as I discovered when I was faced with severe post-natal depression after Amy was born.

I had stayed fit and healthy through my pregnancy, road-running well into the eighth month and, as I have mentioned, leaving work only twelve days before my due date. The house was set and Ash and I were ready, packed and excited as we prepared for our new arrival.

Having struggled so much to have a baby, I was blessed with a healthy pregnancy and an easy birth when, on 15 August 2002, Amy arrived, healthy and beautiful. And then it dawned on me for the first time, as I looked at her in the little see-through plastic crib in the delivery ward, that my life had changed forever.

I just had not been prepared for the overwhelming tsunami of love that literally took my breath away. From that very first moment, I did not want to go back to work. I couldn't go back. I just wanted to be with my baby – every minute.

And to my absolute astonishment, at a moment that I had expected to be full of joy, the heavy, cloying, black clouds of depression settled on me and would not let go.

Of course, as any new parents know, the sleepless nights don't help. And breast-feeding adds a new dimension to anyone trying to keep the show on the road. Because, of course, I was trying to keep on top of things at work too. We were trying to finalise a new marketing campaign for the Virgin One account which, somewhat oddly, involved Hector from the children's television series *Hector's House*. The marketing team came round to my house to show me where they had got to and I was horrified to find that, by the time the meeting had finished, I had been leaking breast milk all over the place. The men were all very understanding, but I was mortified.

To cap it all off, both Amy and I had a dreadful, red, itchy rash from top to toe. For some ludicrous reason, I had decided to change washing powder just when Amy was born and we both had a terrible allergy to it. It took a while to realise the cause and then we had to wash every single thing we possessed again just to get rid of the problem. It sounds funny now, but at the time it just added to my sense of being hopeless, miserable and out of control.

I can still remember looking at my beautiful baby, lying in her cot, one night and wishing it could all be different. That I didn't have to cope. That I could save her from all the horrors and problems of my world and the world in general.

And where, you may ask, was Ash in all this? Well, the truth is that he was there all the time – supportive, worried, cross – just trying to work out what on earth he could do to stop our world being turned upside down. But I don't really remember him during this period at all. It was a time when I felt all alone and where I could survive only by going into myself.

Much to my surprise, and further misery, I could not face listening to music – which has been a great love of mine all my life.

I went to the doctors, and filled in a form designed to analyse how severe my depression was. And it was off the scale.

I was offered medication but refused it because I had seen what that had done to my mum. So I determined to work out what I needed to do to get better and I realised that, somehow, I had to take back control of my life. But that is easier said than done when everything appears to be running faster and faster out of control.

On one occasion, we were staying in my mum and dad's house while they were away and I woke up to check on the baby. She was so quiet and so still that I convinced myself that she was dead and woke Ash up with my screams.

For some reason, I just could not bear being in our house, and we went to stay in France with friends, and to hotels, just to stay sane. I hit rock bottom when, one weekend in a hotel in London, I knew I just could not go back home. For some reason it felt like the walls were coming in on top of me. Looking back now, I suppose it was evidence that I could not just fit my baby into my old life.

So, we set about building a new one.

It was a huge step for me to tell Norman McLuskie that I wanted more time off work. I think I had planned to be away for six weeks but we extended it to just under three months. Norman was, of course, totally supportive, as was Philippa Dickson who was covering my maternity leave. The thing that seemed like a weakness – asking for more time off – turned out to be a strength and it gave me time to plan what to do next.

We put the house on the market and, the day after Amy was christened, we moved into a lovely old farmhouse in a village called Morley, just outside Norwich. The new environment seemed to suit our new life.

Cautiously, I went back to work and managed my hours carefully, having persuaded myself that I would leave my job before the year was out. But somehow, having to focus on getting everything done between nine o'clock in the morning and six o'clock at night made me more efficient. I focused on the real priorities. And I only stayed away from home if I absolutely had to.

I was definitely getting better. But I still could not listen to music. And, when my aunt died, I could not face going to the funeral. By then, though, I had realised that you just have to cut yourself some slack sometimes.

On the other hand, I could not walk away from too many re-sponsibilities. At the end of the day, Ash had given up work and I was the sole breadwinner. And now we had an extra mouth to feed and a new house to pay for. I decided I would just have to take it a day at a time. Do my best. Focus on work when I was there. Focus on the family when at home. Never work at weekends. Take all the help you can get. Get up early and go for a run just to sort out your head in the fresh air.

Over time things got better. I could not pinpoint when. But the music came back, and when, two years later, RBS asked me to move to Scotland we had definitely got through the worst.

The experience changed me and the way that I look at mental health issues today. I had thought that 'depression' was a sign of weakness, an imagined illness, an excuse. Now I know that it is an illness as real as a physical ailment and it needs as much care and repair. Just because we can't see it does not mean it isn't there.

And in the same way as we recover from physical illnesses, we need proactively to find the best solution for our particular problem. If we have a cut, we have to treat it with antiseptic or it will fester. If we have diabetes, we need insulin or we will die. If we have mental health issues, we have to find the right cure. There are all sorts of people – doctors, family, colleagues, friends – who will offer help. My advice would be to take it all. But in the end, in my experience, we do need to take responsibility for our own recovery where we can.

Of course, even that is easier said than done.

Since my battle with post-natal depression, I have had other stressful situations in my life. Buying Northern Rock was hard enough for me to question my own capabilities. Dealing with my Board before floating Virgin Money was sufficient for me to find myself needing to stifle suicidal thoughts. The recent deaths of my parents have again caused me to reflect on a trans-formational life change. But nothing has taken me back right into the depths of post-natal depression with the hopelessness that that brought.

I judge my own mental health these days by my weight. I have battled with it all my life. When I am slim and physically fit, then I am in good shape mentally. And when I am struggling mentally, I decrease the running and increase the chocolate. But, if that is as bad as it gets, then I can manage – despite the wardrobe problems this creates.

In my experience, there is a difference between the clinical depression I felt after Amy was born and the stress that work can bring. I think it is important to differentiate between the two because the first tends to hit you by surprise whereas there are a number of things you can do to defend against work-related stress.

For me, Ash has always put things into perspective. He has always been broadly unimpressed with my world of work – he has always thought there are more important things in life (such as cricket) – and I have always known that, if ever I come home and say, 'Sorry, love, I've had enough and packed it in' or 'Oops – I was fired today', he would say, 'Thank goodness for that – we'll sort it out!'

And that, perversely, has given me real strength to carry on.

If you have more to worry about than work and if you are not putting yourself under pressure to be more and more successful, my experience is that your approach to work can be more authentic. You don't have to make decisions to please anyone else. You don't have to conform to the perceived norms. You can do and say what you think is right. And that is very, very liberating.

Many years ago, I met someone who had been a mentor to Stella Rimington when she was the head of MI5. He asked her how she coped with the pressure and criticism that came to her in her work.

'I know,' she said, 'that the same would happen to whoever sits in this chair. It comes with the job. I don't take it personally.'

Don't take it personally.

That phrase has been a further liberator in my life and has been a means by which I have coped with stress. People are critical of me for a whole host of reasons. If I feel I am genuinely wrong, I will always try and apologise and put myself right. But if it is just a difference of opinion – and I think I am acting with integrity – I push on regardless. It is important, I have found, to be yourself and stick to your guns if you believe you are right.

That way, of course, you find out who your friends really are.

In the City, a lack of conformity has long been criticised. I have been berated by older men. Laughed at by clever bankers. And called unreasonable (at best) by those who haven't been able to cope with the pace of Virgin Money life. And it hurts sometimes, of course.

But what am I to do? Change who I am to please others? Conform to the image of what is acceptable in the City? Give way to the bullies?

No – that is the stuff of nightmares. Because, for me, good mental health comes with knowing who you are. Believing in what you are trying to do. Finding the right place and people to do it with. Listen to the criticism but don't take it personally. Don't be afraid to lose everything to protect your integrity.

I have never told this part of my story before. Stress and depression tend not to feature as conversation topics at City dinners or on anyone's CV. But mental health issues are real and I have no doubt at all that many people deal with issues worse than mine on a very regular basis. They are what make us human and what make us strong.

My advice if it happens to you? Be gentle with yourself and make a plan. Ask for help and accept it with confidence. Throw yourself into your work, your family or the things that matter to you. Make things happen, and make sure those things are good.

And then tell your story, and find like-minded people to work with, laugh with and have fun with along the way. Ignore the detractors and find your supporters. They will make all the difference.

Supporters and Detractors

There is no doubt in my mind that one of the main reasons that Virgin Money has been successful has been our ambition to make everyone better off – EBO.

It was EBO that led us to build Virgin Money Giving and, in turn, that has led us to work with a huge range of charities and good causes.

Add to that the Branson philosophy of 'The answer's "yes" – now what was the question?!', and I often find myself committing to activities that support communities beyond the world of Virgin Money.

And so it was, a few years back, that I was invited to see the plans for a new health centre that was being built in one of the most deprived areas of Scotland – and indeed of the UK. An area where life expectancy is the lowest in the country and where teenage pregnancy is the highest. Where diabetes and obesity drive human suffering and impose a massive strain on the NHS.

So the health centre seemed exactly the right thing to build. But those responsible for it were £100k short of their financial target.

Of course, I said we would find the money. It was a bit impulsive but, as a business, we set aside a pot of money every year for good causes and I hoped this one was good enough.

But I was unable to persuade my Board at the time that this was the right thing to do.

So there I was – a commitment made but unable to pay it from the company. And I just could not afford that amount myself.

I worried a lot about what to do. Letting down the health centre would be devastating for them. Should I take out a loan?

As the deadline loomed, we had a dinner to celebrate the successful listing of Virgin Money on the Stock Exchange and my team hosted a full guest list of bankers, lawyers and accountants.

Before the evening started, one of the bankers was chatting to me and I told him of my £100k dilemma and how it was playing on my mind.

Dinner was good and I didn't notice that a book was being passed around the guests until the very end of the evening – when it was presented to me.

Over dinner my guests had committed to the £100k between them, and that, along with some money from me, meant that the health centre could get off the ground.

It was an amazing moment – and totally unexpected.

It started me thinking about how things happen and where success comes from.

And I am absolutely convinced that it comes by finding your supporters – wherever they may be – and shutting out the detractors, the nay-sayers and those who simply hold you back.

Listen to them for sure. But in the end find those people who lift you with encouragement and support.

I definitely do not mean the 'yes-men'! In my experience they can be as bad as the detractors because they do not add to the dialogue, and that is not support.

For nearly twenty years Dave Dyer has been one of my greatest supporters – yet he has challenged me all the time and shouted at me. A lot. There have been tears and slammed doors. And Virgin Money has always been the better for it.

How has that worked?

Well, broadly, I tend to come up with new thoughts or a plan. Dave will normally say, 'Nope. That won't work because ...' And then, next day, he will come back, normally with some complicated spreadsheet, and say '... but if we looked at it like this I think it could work.'

Building on each other's thoughts and ideas, not closing them down – that, in my view, is the way to innovation, development and success.

Brian Pitman was a supporter of mine in a different way. When, during the financial crisis, so many people – politicians, regulators, journalists – wanted to ask him for his views, he would go to see them and to contribute to the debate – but he would always take me with him. Not only did I learn more than I could ever have expected just by listening to those discussions, but I could never have expected to meet the people he introduced me to on my own. He opened doors to me that otherwise would have remained closed.

Mervyn King was different again. Once we were the confirmed acquirer of Northern Rock, he called me in to see him at the Bank of England. He told me what was expected of me, of course. I can't really remember all that. But what I do remember is his story about his Australian friend who had not been back to the UK for over thirty years. When he returned to the UK, he said, 'Mervyn – since I've been gone, the supermarkets are transformed. Products, displays, cleanliness, quality. But the banks. They haven't changed one jot.'

'And that,' Mervyn King said to me, 'is your challenge.'

I have never forgotten that guidance.

Sometimes, just asking for a piece of work to be done is enough support – it shows confidence in you. When George Osborne invited me to take on the Women in Finance work, I could never have imagined how many doors that would open and how many new people I would meet.

Investors are the same. In my view, the best are those who encourage long-term performance. Only last Christmas I got a card from an important investor – thanking me and the Virgin Money team 'for working tirelessly on behalf of your shareholders'. It doesn't take much, but it is appreciated and remembered.

It lifts you up.

I shall take little space here writing about the detractors. But there have been many. Those who try and close us down. Those who say no or go slow. The critics who have never run a business.

I see them as if they are the dementors of the Harry Potter books. They enter a room and darkness falls. Your energy is sucked out of you.

Years ago, I was in an MBA class feeling inspired, as always, by my tutor Ronnie Lessem, who makes me believe that I can change the world. Ronnie would continually challenge the established norms and many students simply derided him – and me, whenever I built on his ideas. They would roll their eyes and look skywards at my interventions. On this particular occasion I left a two-day session saying that I looked forward to seeing everyone again soon.

'Not if we see you first,' said a senior man from Sainsbury Homebase.

I couldn't believe the easy cruelty of the jibe and have never forgotten it, even though he was as good as his word and I have never seen him since.

When we bought Northern Rock, a number of people took some pleasure in telling me how the previous management team were sure that the Virgin Money team would fail. Who knows how true that was? But I was delighted to see Gary Hoffman – the previous CEO of Northern Rock – in the audience at a recent speech I gave in London. He stayed afterwards and thanked me for what we had done with Northern Rock – generous words that made me feel good.

And when I flew back from Necker Island in 2014 with plans for the early listing of Virgin Money, I knew I had to pick my supporters carefully to make it happen. Lee, in particular, would take a lot of persuading to accept such an ambitious plan with such challenging deadlines in double-quick time.

But sometimes you just have to ignore the negative voices. The trick, of course, is to find more supporters than detractors.

I think that is sometimes hard for women in particular. We are often brought up with certain expectations on us – perhaps to be a good wife or a good mother. To be less determined than men. To behave nicely and to be feminine.

There is often nothing more discouraging for a woman than to hear that she is 'scary' or 'emotional' or 'hormonal' – trust me, I have heard it all.

I remember exactly how I felt, years ago, when Philip Scott, my boss at the time, told me that I could be brilliant – if only I was less emotional. Well, of course we don't want people weeping all over the boardroom tables, but I do think we need people with passion saying what they believe.

I recall, all too well, as we tried to resolve our Board issues by creating a planned crisis in early 2014, that someone asked me if I was behaving oddly because of the menopause!

But the good news is that I have had many, many more supporters in my career so far than detractors. Or at least, if I haven't, I have pushed the detractors so far to the back of my mind that I barely remember them.

That said, supporters also need to be genuine. I know that it might be deemed a quaint and naïve thought in the City, but loyalty means a lot to me. So I was particularly surprised when a banker with whom I had worked closely throughout our listing kept turning up on the other side of potential future deals. He took me out for a drink one night and was clearly surprised that I did not like that behaviour. 'Why do you think I should be on your side?' he asked. I was so taken aback that I did not have an immediate reply.

'Because you're my broker' was the obvious reply, which only came to me after he had left.

In the end, we all need to know who we can trust. Who is on our side. Who has our back.

I am extremely fortunate to have had Richard Branson as such a big supporter. He has trusted us with his brand, his bank and his future – and at every twist and turn he has come through. The answer has always been 'yes'.

And that is why, in the end, health centres get built, banks get rescued and the world gets better.

The answer's 'yes'. Now – what was the question?

AFTERWORD

I AM WRITING the final words for this book on a flight from London Heathrow to Glasgow.

As I came out of the airport lounge, quite by chance, I bumped into Alastair Gornall, whose words, support and introductions over the years have made much of this story possible.

I told him I was writing this book and that he features in it.

'Do I?' he exclaimed. 'Hope it's nice!'

'It's odd,' I said. 'As the book developed I realised that, although there have been tough times, as I look back over the years, only the positive stuff is important.'

I surprised myself when I said that. You hear so often how we all learn from our mistakes and from the tough times. There is no doubt that is true – but almost certainly only when success of some sort follows the crisis.

There is no point in wallowing in problems – celebrating success and moving on is one of the key messages of this book.

When Richard Branson and I met with Norman McLuskie and Fred Goodwin in the Orangery in Holland Park to discuss the sale of the Virgin One account to RBS, Richard asked Fred when we could expect a book about the NatWest deal. 'Never,' he said. 'It's about looking forward now.'

Richard, on the other hand, while being the ultimate visionary – looking to this planet and beyond – has written many books on his adventures and learnings so far.

So, why was this book ready to be written now?

Well, 2016 was a year of change.

That year both of my parents died exactly nineteen weeks apart. My mother's death was quick and unexpected, my father's following the painful trauma of cancer.

They lived full lives and spent the last ten years living with us as part of our extended family – instilling some old-fashioned values into Amy and sharing some of our adventures along the way.

I thought I knew everything about them, but following their deaths there are questions I still have, to which I will never know the answer. So, after the death of my parents, and prompted by Kevin Revell, I thought I should just jot down this story as a sort of *aide-mémoire* for me and a record for Amy along the way.

I found that, once I started, I couldn't stop. It all flowed without any reference to diaries, colleagues or media – social or otherwise. As a result, it is my memory alone of events that have happened over many years. I believe the stories here to be entirely accurate and none have been polished for effect.

The point, I think, is that they are the stories as I experienced them. The stories that got me and Virgin Money to this point today.

They ignore or only lightly touch upon so many other events that have been important to me. Understanding a completely new culture as one half of a mixed marriage. Getting involved in charity work. Receiving a CBE in 2014. Experiencing IVF. Becoming involved in the political sphere through my membership of David Cameron's Business Advisory Group and other committees. Coming to terms with the consequences and opportunities of Brexit. Maybe these are stories for another day.

The common theme of the Virgin Money story is an unswerving belief in EBO – that business has a duty to contribute to a better society, a duty to strive to make everyone better off and an imperative to stand up and make a difference.

I have been very fortunate to have been given the privilege of running a Virgin business for so long. Richard Branson has always stood up for business as a force for good and is the most authentic example of EBO that you can have.

And the Virgin brand also stands for something beyond business. It stands for doing things better. Challenging the status quo. Championing the consumer. And having fun.

And maybe that's why, when I look back over the story so far, it is the good, the fun and the exciting stuff that I remember best. It is what inspires us and drives us to the next impossible dream.

Because, as I look back over the last twenty years or so at Virgin, I realise that I could never have imagined, back then, what a journey we would have been on and what we could have achieved.

We have done that by not taking no for an answer. By not being deflected by criticism. By asking the stupid question – every time. By building networks and making friends. By creating a movement of people that want banking to be better. By creating a common purpose of making everyone better off.

And we have only just started. I am looking forward to the next stage of the journey – and wherever that takes us.

Postscript

Some of the key characters in this story are no longer with us.

Mark Barnes, the most charming and positive force of nature you could imagine, died in a car crash in 2001. He left family, friends and colleagues who have taken years to come to terms with his passing.

Andrew Sage, the brilliant mathematician with the ability to present complex concepts in very simple ways, died in 2006 after a difficult battle with cancer. You don't meet people like Andrew very often in your life, and it was a privilege to work with him.

Geoff Walker, the epitome of kindness and care, who managed to keep us legal and compliant while still being innovative, and who was loved by all of us, died suddenly at his home in 2007. He left a gap that we have never really managed to fill again in our business.

Philippa Dickson, who was so supportive to me personally and to the business while I adjusted to becoming a mother, passed away at home in 2016, after a long and brave fight against cancer.

Brian Pitman told me rich and colourful stories as we walked around London together during the financial crisis. I asked him if he would write a book. 'I will – one day,' he said. That day never came and we have lost the opportunity to learn more from a wise man and an experienced banker.

ACKNOWLEDGEMENTS

THANKS TO everyone at Virgin Money and the Virgin Group, without whom this book would never have been written. And special thanks to Kevin Revell for the hours spent getting it ready for publication.

WHAT HAPPENED WHEN

1995
Virgin Direct opens for business in partnership with Norwich Union.

1996
Pensions, life insurance, critical illness and unit trust products are launched.

1997
Australian Mutual Provident Society (AMP) acquire a 50 per cent stake in Virgin Direct from Norwich Union. First £1 billion of funds under Virgin Direct management.

1998
Virgin One account, a joint venture with the Royal Bank of Scotland Group (RBS), is launched.

2001
RBS acquire Virgin and AMP stakes in the Virgin One account to own the business outright. RBS acquire National Westminster Bank.

2002
Virgin Money launches first Virgin credit card in partnership with MBNA.

2003
Virgin Money launches in Australia.

2004
Virgin Group takes 100 per cent control of Virgin Money.

2005
RBS opens a new head office in Gogaburn, Edinburgh.

2006
Virgin Money launches the Virgin Money credit card in South Africa.

2007
Team return to Virgin Money.
Northern Rock suffers the first run
on a UK bank for many years.

2008
Nationalisation of Northern Rock.

2009
Virgin Money Giving launches.

2010
Virgin Money acquires regional bank
Church House Trust. US investor
Wilbur Ross (W.L. Ross & Co.)
invests £100 million in Virgin Money.

2011
Virgin Money agrees to acquire
Northern Rock plc.

2012
Northern Rock becomes part
of Virgin Money.

2013
Virgin Money acquires a £1 billion
portfolio of credit-card assets from
MBNA.

2014
Virgin Money lists on the London
Stock Exchange. The Virgin
Money Foundation is launched.

2015
Migration of assets to Virgin Money's
new credit-card platform is completed.

2016
HM Treasury report 'Empowering
Productivity: Harnessing the Talents
of Women in Financial Services'
is launched.

PHOTO CREDITS

Section 1

1. *Hello!* Magazine
2. Top: Virgin Money; bottom: Reuters/Luke McGregor
3. Author's own
4. Getty
5. Virgin Money

6–7. Murdo MacLeod

8. Author's own

Section 2

1. Top: Virgin Money; bottom: author's own
2. Top: Suc Flood; bottom: Virgin Money
3. Virgin Money
4. Top: author's own; bottom: Virgin Money
5. Top: author's own; bottom: *Daily Mail*
6. Top: Virgin Limited Edition; bottom: Virgin Money
7. Top: Virgin Money; bottom: Sinead Clarke
8. Top: The Financial Times/Daniel Jones; bottom: author's own

INDEX